The Films of Mae West

The Films of Mae West

by Jon Tuska

Intrduction by Parker Tyler

The Citadel Press
Secaucus, N. J.

For
DAN *and* AUDREY

The author wishes to express here his special gratitude to the following people who were vitally instrumental in making this book possible in its present form.

To MCA-Universal; Gene F. Giaquinto, Vice President, Universal Pictures; the late Irving Weiner, Universal Pictures; Ernest B. Goodman, MCA Television Legal Department; Maryka DeHand, MCA International; Hania Kuzmik, United World Films; Audrey Foster, formerly of MCA Television, Chicago; Daniel A. Bishop, formerly of Universal 16, Chicago.

To Columbia Pictures Corporation; Sid Weiner, Administrative Director of Screen Gems; Joe Abruscato, Screen Gems; Ronnie Steadwell, formerly Screen Gems' publicity; Merrie Thomas, Screen Gems' publicity; Bob Nilsen, Screen Gems' traffic.

To 20th Century-Fox Film Corporation; Blackmer Johnson, Officer, Legal Department; 20th Century-Fox publicity.

To Films, Inc; Allen Green, Vice President; Gordon Anderson, traffic; Douglas A. Lemza, Rediscovery Librarian.

To Paramount Pictures Corporation.

To NBC Radio Archives.

To Movie Star News, Paula Klaw; to Vitaprint, New York; to The Memory Shop, New York; to Larry Edmunds' Bookstore, Hollywood; to Cinemabilia, Ernest Burns, New York.

To Miles Kreuger, Leonard Maltin, and countless readers of earlier versions of this material in *Views & Reviews* Magazine.

To MISS MAE WEST.

First edition
Copyright ©1973 by Jon Tuska
All rights reserved
Published by Citadel Press
A division of Lyle Stuart, Inc.
120 Enterprise Ave., Secaucus, N. J. 07094
Manufactured in the United States of America by Halliday Lithograph Corp., West Hanover, Mass.
Library of Congress catalog card number: 73-84149
ISBN 0-8065-0377-7

Title spread: With Russell Hopton in *I'm No Angel*

Contents

Intrduction by Parker Tyler

Reading this book by Jon Tuska, I became nothing but prejudice: pleasurable prejudice. The art of biography is a flexible thing. On one hand it represents the life story of an individual, on the other a collective portrait of the human race. A biography that is too critical of its subject, or hostile toward him or her, can hardly claim to be classifiable as a biography; moreover, a biography which seems to overrate or underrate the human race as such cannot be expected to prove justly appreciative, or justly critical, of the race's particular member who is its subject. I see that the author of this account of Mae West's personality, career and fame did not stop to consider the above-mentioned problems. If he had, he might have written a more critical book, a more speculative book, but not one, as this is, so devoted, so whole of heart, so humanly valid.

This book is a tribute in the most absolute sense of the word. It seems to go beyond all measurements—or rather to be, like Mae West herself, a singular standard to which nothing is relevant but itself. Most authors, biographers or whatever, give instance to considerations of style, precedents and standards in the same field, such as the possibilities and restraints of language. Mr. Tuska has tactically ignored such encumbering elements and allowed his admiration for his subject to immerse him in the business of telling everything he considers of importance about her. And there is more of that, be sure, than you may have suspected. A sublime simplicity invests this book. And curiously, it is the same simplicity that seems to have governed the celebrated being we all know, to our joy and profit, as Mae West, woman, actress and movie star.

Superficially, these terms do about everything to define Mae as an individual. Yet take the first: woman. Isn't it actually redundant because simply self-evident? Of course, when one spontaneously thus classifies someone, it usually means, tacitly, *plain* woman, *typical* woman, *just* woman . . . a woman like anyone else of her sex. Yet consider this: Doesn't Mae West, as both a sex and an individual, go beyond such a designation? Is she not more than a woman? And I don't mean, as I myself and others before this have implied, and stated, that Mae West is a Hollywood goddess, and thus more than a woman in that sense. Surely, she is one of the sex goddesses in an idiom that is commonly accepted and that, I daresay, I had my share in promoting. Still, I don't mean just that, and if Mr. Tuska himself duly terms Mae a sex goddess, he does so because nowadays it is a natural convention; virtually the same as calling her a woman. Virtually the same, I say, but just as inadequate!

And why should it be inadequate? Take the second and third designations given above: actress and movie star. These are merely the types by which a woman (actress) and a first-rank film professional (movie star) are known. It is quite as natural as referring to Elizabeth (Queen) or Nixon (President). It is only one of the things that inheres in the given uniqueness that is an individual. Basically it conveys information in the biographic-dictionary manner (West, Mae) and is a formal convention like the alphabetical order making it easy to look up subjects in the index of a book. Much to be preferred is one good, long look at Mae West, the being we have known through the years of her beginnings and her rising career, and now when she is one who, in that classic and deathless phrase, rests on her laurels. This book certainly achieves one good, very good, long look. Jon Tuska, as I just hinted, has not allowed the usual literary scruples to complicate his look. Never taking his eyes off his subject, he planted his feet firmly on the ground—wide enough apart to gain confident leverage—grasped all the facts within his extensive reach, and swallowed them whole. This method is, in its way, a special art. Its dividends are—again like Mae West herself—incalculable as well as extremely tangible.

In modern times the star personality is such a known quantity that one need not lean on the distinction between a *star* and an *actress* or *actor*. Everybody understands the difference without its affecting one's esteem for the object of one's adoration. Yet, like Garbo and Charlie Chaplin, Mae is (or was, for she is pretty much retired these days) a gifted performer, thoroughly trained in projecting whatever she elected to project. Hence, one good long look at her means taking in, in a single charged glance, both the star and the actress; it means instantaneously enveloping with one's imagination the quantity we glibly call, in Mae West as in others, the star personality. Doing that now, I find that a curious thing happens. Suddenly, those formal divisions I mentioned fade away. No longer is there any difference between the private Mae and the public Mae, between Mae as a screen image and Mae as a person having, necessarily, physical quantity and weight. Mae West, perhaps even more than Garbo, has a way of notifying the "human being" with which nature has supplied the world, and that undoubtedly exists, of her irrelevance: *she* has nothing to do, really, with the tremendous creation that is Mae West the great star. I mean, of course, not the Mae West that a few friends and personal associates and her studio and her director know, but the Mae West that *everybody* knows.

So everything we learn here about Mae in her early days as a performer—when she was very young before and after the First World War and played in Broadway musicals—comes as a special surprise, something almost incredible because downright bizarre. For most of her fans, Mae exists permanently as a series of heroines perpetually reincarnated on the television screen: Lady Lou of **She Done Him Wrong**, Tira of **I'm No Angel**, Ruby of **Belle of the Nineties**, Cleo of **Goin' to Town**, the Frisco Doll of **Klondike Annie**, Mavis of **Go West, Young Man** and Flower Belle of **My Little Chickadee**. . . . The list is incomplete but the continuity is perfect. Cannily, Mr. Tuska skips Mae's childhood, which he says has been taken care of, anyway, in Mae's autobiography, **Goodness Had Nothing to Do With It**. Deliberately, his book concentrates on Mae's public career. Thinking of Mae as a star personality, it seems purely coincidental that she ever had a childhood, a youth, a budding career, that she had to struggle with small parts, smalltime theatre and (far from being a star) was just another member of the cast striving to be noticed. *Variety*, one of her severest critics, even chided her for trying to make her act "bigtime." Yet all those things, quite typical of success stories in the theatrical profession, were true; they unquestionably really happened to Mae. With a shock of amused delight, almost with a gasp, I find that Mae was once an earnest young thing bent on singing and dancing and adding to her repertory of talents, and that, thus intensely preoccupied,

she was billed in a production of Florenz Ziegfeld, Jr., *Winsome Widow* ("a comedy with music in three acts") as La Petite Daffy!! That fully deserves, I think, an extra exclamation point. And the year, if you please, was 1912: a fact that is its own exclamation point. Noting that a "May West" is listed in the cast of several burlesque shows, Mr. Tuska warily declares it uncertain whether Mae actually ever performed in burlesque. I guess she never precisely admitted it; although why not, if true, it is hard to guess.

The dance scholar can detect certain style mannerisms such as Mae's induplicable swagger—a sort of slow rhythmic counterpoint operating between shoulders and hips—as traceable to the jaunty strut of the burlesque stage. To be sure, at one point of pre-World War I times, Mae had to ask someone what another dancer, whom she was watching, was doing. The answer was: "She's shakin' the shimmy." Mae immediately mastered this art and introduced it into her own act. This may have been the origin of what was called the shimmy shawabble, which it is quite certain that Mae performed because she herself says that the first time she did the shimmy, she "tore down the house." She was then in vaudeville, and already in her repertory, Mr. Tuska notes, was "the bump." Surely, without violating the proprieties, he might have added, "and the grind."

That Mae got some bad reviews should disturb nobody, least of all Mae herself. She knew her business, and its future, better than anyone else did. *Variety* spoke of her in *Winsome Widow* as a "rough soubret who did a 'Turkey' just a bit too coarse for this $2.00 audience." Well, it is significant that, as Mae came on and on and on, *Variety* changed its mind. The New York *Herald Tribune* called her chorus-girl characterization "capital" although marred toward the close by "vulgarity." Nevertheless, when her shimmy shawabble had a resounding success, *Variety* capitulated by formulating the then state of her future immortal image as "the rough hand on hip character . . . that she first conceived as the ideal type of woman single in vaudeville." Already, she was in history and thenceforward she began making it to suit herself. "Woman single"? Yes! And one of the greatest that ever existed.

My point is that this inspiration—this idea of a female type so grand and unique that it could become a star personality—is the where and the how, and even the why, of Mae West's "birth." One can no more think of Mae as a child than one can think of Shirley Temple as a woman. By all means, we know Mae had to be a child to get to be a woman; that was fully as natural as that, to get to be a woman, Shirley Temple had first to be a child. On the other hand, the way in which we think of the mythological beings called movie stars is all that matters in any question concerning origins. It is something that happens, whenever their names are mentioned, like magic. Automatically, a dynamic image leaps into focus, whole and final, without past or future, and simply carrying the profound vibration we name Eternity. It's only natural to think of Charlie Chaplin as wearing a mustache and derby while in the cradle and afterwards, and of Shirley Temple as everlastingly, unalterably, the incredibly mature moppet sporting doll's curls, a smile and a pout, and built remarkably like a chubby little girl who can sing and dance like a grown-up professional.

I can quote Mae's own words to justify my view of her. "My basic style has never changed," she said. "I couldn't [change it] if I wanted to. I am a captive of myself. It or I created a Mae West and neither of us could let the other go, or would want to." That is why it seems impossible to separate Mae's image from the invisibly joined bra and girdle, the marcelled wig, the provocative curl of the sweet mouth, the hippy sway with perched hand, as though they were things carved in the marble of the Venus de Milo. As with the origin of the goddess Athena, who sprang full-blown—myth says—from the forehead of her father, Zeus, Mae seems to have achieved birth without the help of a female parent, or with no help, as she says, but her own. One might think of her rolling into undulant step before us from *her own forehead*. However, one should add that the instrument effecting this remarkable feat was surely not (as reputed in the case of Athena) an axe . . . No! The instrument was something, I would hazard, much nicer in Mae's case.

Through modern culture, personal identity has acquired an aura of difficult ambiguity, and in the domain of the psychological clinic, identity may be a thing hanging in suspense and desperately pursued. One can think of Mae as being desperately pursued by men, but certainly not as pursuing (she had a marvelous hauteur even when inwardly smitten by a man) and doubly not pursuing a personal possession such as an "identity." Some people (so a modern myth goes) spend a lifetime pursuing their "identity." To possess hers, Mae took only as long as it takes a woman to secrete folding money in her bosom. Folding money, after a certain point, was something that never left Mae.

Pondering Mae's immutability, I am reminded of Salvador Dali's magnificent portrait of her, a work for which she did not need to "sit." Dali doubtless used a photograph for its basis and what he did was to interpret her face, seen frontally in a familiar expression, in terms of a rather grand room on two levels. Instantly recognizing her, one perceives her chin defined by four rounding steps leading to the second, or main, level of the "room." Her lips, just as neatly illusioned, are a sumptuous violet-red sofa, her nose (only its blunt uplifted tip and wide nostrils visible) a fireplace against a solid red wall opposite us, and her eyes two gold-framed pictures made to look like dark cityscapes as much as like eyes. Two jeweled pendants serve as realistic earrings while divided, voluptuously billowing drapes (making a stagelike proscenium for the "room") constitute a marvelous illusion of Mae's wavy, white-blonde hair. Strangely, the red wall serves as a sort of half-mask, but this seems to add to, rather than detract from, the utter conviction of this portrait. How many faces, even of other very great stars, could survive such a portrayal? Yet in Mae's case, her identity not only remains intact, the whole effect of it is astonishingly lifelike.

Is Dali's portrait in any sense or degree frivolous or disrespectful? Quite the contrary. Dali may be a very deep joker at times but he is beyond question a serious person. So am I. However much I sometimes speak in jesting irony or high camp, I mean everything I say in perfect earnestness. When I was a growing intellectual, it was fashionable to think Mae West interesting because she made sex "funny". But that was just the danger. She made it so funny that one might lose sight of the splendor of its underlying seriousness. Once I ran into a woman writer who told me that, some years before, she had interviewed Mae West.

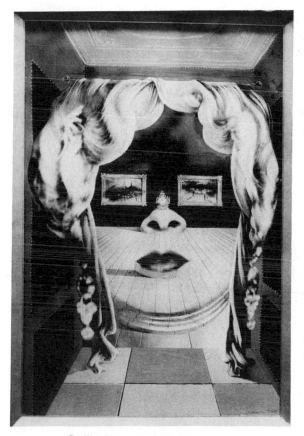

Dali's famous conception

One of the questions she put to her was how she reacted to the fact that a certain film critic (myself) had compared her to a female impersonator.

My confidante reported to me how Mae had responded: "All I want to know is this: was he *for* me or *against* me?" Though I understood the interviewer had assured Mae that I was for her, I want to take this opportunity of saying it for myself: "Mae, I was, and am, for you! And I'm for you because I think of you so seriously." Let me confess here to other things I've termed Mae West and give the ultimate why of my various impressions and epithets. It was in 1944 that I published the passage about Mae as suggesting a female impersonator.* As I am reminded from time to time, the point has not been forgotten.

Mr. Tuska writes of Mae's fascination for inverts by quoting her own words. "I've always had it, dear," she told someone. "They're crazy about me 'cause I give 'em a chance to play. My characterization is sexy and with humor and they like to imitate me, the things I say, the way I say 'em, the way I move. It's easy for 'em to imitate me 'cause the gestures are exaggerated, flamboyant, *sexy*, and that's what they wanna look like, feel like, and I've stood up for 'em. They're good kids. I don't like the police abusin' 'em, and in New York I told 'em, 'When you're hittin' one of those guys, you're hittin' a woman, 'cause a born homosexual is a female in a male body.'" That's magnificent common sense, and up to a point quite true. But, adorable though it be as a sentiment, it applies primarily to female impersonators and, as we know very well, not all male homosexuals are female impersonators.

That Mae, in the above words, was not indulging in late second thoughts or idle vaunting, is proven by Mr. Tuska's faithful scholarship in recording the details of **The Drag**, a play Mae wrote and had produced in 1926, and that, as the title indicates, is largely about female impersonators. It was premiered in Bridgeport, Conn., and did not reach New York because a panel of city officials and members of the medical profession declined to endorse it. Mr. Tuska alleges that "some thirty gay people" were in it, many of them in the drag sequence. For 1926, that was an audacious no less than a prophetic and gallant gesture by Mae. The truth is that her above statement applies to the transsexual compulsion of certain homosexuals who may or may not have the Myra Breckinridge complex and desire a sex change. As the film critic explicitly named by Gore Vidal as Myra's inspiration, I might be said to have privileged testimony on this subject. In fact, Myra herself is an atypical or offbeat female impersonator, not content to be "a female in a male body." *Chacun à son goût!* Fate having given Mae herself a female body, she had no such problem.

In later books and articles, I called Mae "Mother Superior of the Faggots," "the White Goddess in metaphysically transsexual drag," and (crystallizing my remarks made in 1944) "the Great Mother of the Homosexual Son." Therefore I am not among those film critics cited by Mr. Tuska as having "insisted" that Mae "was [*sic*] a female impersonator." To help prove her genuineness, Mr. Tuska incidentally reproduces her marriage certificate. I would be the last to question the authenticity of that document although it is only a proof of the fact

* THE HOLLYWOOD HALLUCINATION

that someone named Mae West was once legally married.

Obviously those special terms of mine for Mae were *figurative*. Figurative speech simply denotes essences where literal speech denotes facts. Mae is no more a female impersonator in fact than (we are to take it) she was, while in a position to be so, a mother in fact. Any figure of speech denotes functions of mind and emotion rather than facts to be verified in the flesh. No man has yet been a mother, yet a man may be said to mother his children if his wife has died or abandoned her family. Impressions of people based on figures of speech refer to personality and style—and Mae has lots of both. I mean, in sum, that there is a supercharged dimension of reality where certain functions are refined and condensed in forms which do not correspond to natural forms but rather to psychological and moral forms; in brief, to symbolic forms.

An example exists in Mae's own career. After her second starring vehicle from Paramount, **I'm No Angel**, Mae, already a divinity of the cult-lovers, posed as the Statue of Liberty for *Vanity Fair*, a famous culture mag of a bygone day of chic. The alert George Jean Nathan remarked of this image that it looked more like "the Statue of Libido." That was a nice period wisecrack yet too symbolistic to be really satisfying as a truth. Mae *did* carry a torch for the opposite sex but she didn't hold it up, even figuratively, in her right hand. Left or right, the hand held it, restlessly, suggestively and literally, on one hip. Mae, incidentally, was short in stature, but her proportions were right and so theatrical illusion gave her an extraordinary scale.

Correctly, Mr. Tuska emphasizes Mae's insistence on sexuality in general as perfectly healthy. I would be the last to quarrel with that. My point is that the Mae West cult is to be explained by claims greater than any she herself or even her most valiant champion, Mr. Tuska, has made. As for sex from the pornographic angle of theatrical performance, Mae herself has put the record straight for all time by remarking (as Mr. Tuska pertinently reveals) that sexual obscenity is as nothing compared to "the enormous obscenity that is war." Bravo, Mae! Inevitably, the moral healthiness of sex invokes issues other than those contained in Mae's films and plays. But she had a hidden angle even on such corollary matters.

We live in a time of strong minority movements meant to liberate underdog groups. One of the sex-group movements is Women's Liberation. I get a thrill just from contemplating what might happen if Mae ever tangled, on some hypothetic TV talk show, with Gloria Steinem or Betty Friedan. Actually, I think modern women have more to learn about sex from Mae West than from Kate Millett, Germaine Greer and Jill Johnston combined. A problem in the fem-lib movement as it stands is lesbianism, some factionalists maintaining that lesbianism is the very heart of equality with men, others that it is the shoals on which the sex-equality aim of women might well founder. How the idea that lesbianism could achieve either of those antithetic functions should make Mae laugh! And I think I understand the reason she *would* laugh.

Mae's whole style as a sex symbol was based on sexual play as the game of getting your man. This game, as everyone is aware, can be played by women quite heartlessly—it can be played by them, sadistically and dishonestly, as a way of triumphing over the opposite sex by snaring it and then cheating it or jilting it. This is why, in the film made of **Myra Breckinridge**, Mae's appearance in the role of Letitia Van Allen had even more point than the same character in the novel. Letitia represents the opposite of Myra's insane fem-lib desire to humiliate the male by, in effect, flirting with him and then heartlessly raping him. If Mae in her films flirted with a man heartlessly, she did so for ulterior reasons, and basically because she wasn't in the least attracted to him. Of course, such moves in the game depended technically on the plot of this or that film. But underneath, Mae changed her affections (when she did so) honestly; she gave her heart wholly even when her game of sex-tactics made her play hard to get. This was something that no *plot incident* made plain but that her *style as a woman* made plain. It was stamped on her image like the regally sexy lilt to her walk, the hand on her hip, the studied toughness that was all-over silk, the tightlipped, loaded smirk that went with her nasal, softly intoned "Come up an' see me sometime!" It was visible on her whenever her glance swept a man from head to toe and then, if she liked what she saw, grappled with him eye-to-eye.

The ethic understood by women who are fem-lib champions is that to play the sex game, any style, is to play invariably into the hands of the male enemy. Why? Because, we are told, society and its present economics are structured so that in the end the female, by the very token that she gets her man, will be victimized by the male-dominated system. Thus have come about the efforts of women to change the rules of a game that at last means, so they think, utter "surrender" to the opposite sex in bed. Such liberated modern women believe that females are bound to lose in bed, no matter how much they look like winners there. Now—as I am sure Mae West would agree—this fatalistic gloom about heterosexuality from the woman's side is entirely a state of mind, and this state of mind is one that automatically rejects the male as an all-powerful sex object. When women complain nowadays of being "only" sex objects for men, it apparently does not occur to them that, if they wanted to enough, they could turn the tables on men by making sex objects of *them*. Why not? All a woman has to do, as Mae knows so well, is to desire them enough. After her Hollywood career petered out, Mae demonstrated in just what sense she regarded men as sex objects by touring with a nightclub act in which she was attended by a bevy of sensational muscle men whose main function, besides posing, was to present their biceps for her to feel.

So far as lesbianism goes, certain modern lesbians look freaky because their sexual inclination is due not so much to loving women as to hating men; and if men are hated, they are hated first (according to fem-lib rules) as economic, not as sexual, rivals. Not love or sex, but a job and its economic independence, are frequently at stake; and something that is to be called, perhaps, sex-ego pride. Surely, I don't deny that men may play the sex game as heartlessly as women sometimes do. But all risk in anything to be called a sex game is mutually sustained by whichever sexes be involved. The decisive thing, homosexually or heterosexually, is the degree of inner commitment to sexual desire for a specific object.

With her sister Beverly in the mid-twenties

With Mme. Helena Rubinstein

With Billy Sunday, the evangelist, and his wife on the set of *She Done Him Wrong*

Here is where Mae enters, triumphantly, as a sex goddess: she is thus identifiable fully as much because she is a *desiring subject* as because she is a *desirable object*. This is what her "style" conveys and what links her, basically and indissolubly, with the homosexual who is a female impersonator. *His* inner commitment is the same as Mae's; that is, his desire for the male is so great, so finally decisive, that dressing like a woman is simply the outward token of a perfect inner commitment. Simply by existing as an image, his masquerade gives advance notice to the desired male that the readiest of commitments is present and active. The reason that Mae suggests a female impersonator, then, is not that so many of them imitate her (which they do, in fact, mostly as camp) but that her commitment to the male is, like theirs, uncommonly utter. Most women have too much ego-pride to let men know in advance how attractive they are by advertising it in terms of articulate reactions. Mae's glance, her swinging swagger, her total physical insinuation, amount to a dance of love-gestures. Ego-proud women, on the other hand, are unsure, not so much of their own sex appeal, as of the sex appeal of the men whom they elect to find attractive. Mae was never unsure about those things: either her own attractiveness or a man's.

Nature formed Mae's mature figure to look not only reassuringly maternal but reassuringly Victorian, suggesting old-fashioned times when sex in women was a simpler proposition, less of a moral problem, more of a known quantity. Mae's well-packed curves made men think of their mothers, not in particular but in general; specifically, that is, of a greatly liberated mother, one that would cheerfully forgive her son the most grievous fault just because of *what he is*. His assurance of this is all in an image: Mae is warm, ever-ready, essentially maternal love cast in the shape of caressive and caressible flesh . . . flesh generous of quantity, cozily creviced, in every way, and at every point, available and unstinted. . . .

And that, being that, is a very great deal! Consider that what is most negotiable between the sexes in bed is not always what is most negotiable in the imagination. Like the Letitia Van Allen that Mae plays in **Myra Breckinridge**, she promised a man the world simply by existing; if she also promised it verbally, that merely added something beautiful to the style of the promise—the way the ornamental clock placed by Dali in his portrait of Mae, on the mantelpiece formed by her nose, adds to her identity an exquisite fillip of camp. . . . Thus Mae's divine secret is the same as Aphrodite's: she appeals first, and omnipotently, to the sexual imagination. It is the function of every love goddess since time began. She makes not just men but everybody think of what *she* is thinking of: sex. And we know she's thinking of it not so much because of what she may do or say as because of the precise images she makes doing it, the precise sounds she makes staying it. These things coalesced into an unforgettable style. Is there any particular description for this style?

Try this: "I ain't ice," Mae is tersely quoted by Mr. Tuska. No. She is fire—in the underbrush of the flesh. Tropical. Hot with rain. Like a miraculous orchid no one had ever seen before. Or this: Having received threats against her person soon after arriving in Hollywood, she appeared in public with four bodyguards—two of them to hold her, I daresay, two to hold back the crowd. She went thus accompanied to prizefights. At one of these, she met Cary Grant and wanted him for leading man in her first picture. She got him.

By that last sentence, I hope not to give the impression that I believe Mae, outside working hours, thought of nothing but rounding up males in singles and groups! Without doubt, she though of Cary Grant as she did of herself—as an image that meant a special sex style. As for giving mere men much of her time, or making love in earnest, a *star* cannot afford to do that. Mae was conventional in this regard—over and over her chronicler, Mr. Tuska, is sensitive to this point—she was an ultra among star personalities: very conscious of her vocation as time-absorbing and self-absorbing. In an interview with *Playboy*, Mae spoke up once and for all in behalf of what might be called her artistic conscience: "I concentrate on myself most of the time; that's the only way a person can become a star in the true sense. I never wanted a love that meant surrender of my self-possession. I saw what it did to other people when they loved another person the way I loved myself, and I didn't want that problem. I had to stay in command of my career."

It was, I suppose, exactly that personal air of being "in command" that made me write, not long ago, that Mae's "suavity is that of a candid diplomat" and her "tacit authority is that of the Commander in Chief of the Armed Forces."

With Gary Cooper celebrating the repeal of Prohibition

I ventured once to suggest that the liberation of women and their new-won sexual freedom had so altered men's views on the importance of chastity that jealousy was no longer a theme for tragedy, but only for comedy; but this observation was received with so much indignation that I will not enlarge upon it.

—W. Somerset Maugham

Foreword

This book is about Mae West's entertainment career, which can be said to have begun when she was seven years old and which is still going on today. I have made no attempt to tell the story of her childhood beyond the biographical sketch in the chapter on her early theatrical work. She has written of it, as best it will likely be done, in her autobiography *Goodness Had Nothing to Do With It* which has recently been published in an enlarged and revised edition by Macfadden-Bartell Corporation. I would recommend reading it, should anyone desire to know the more intimate details of her youth.

My concern is with Mae West's career and with the impact that career has had. Mae West's public life as an entertainer is enormously interesting and provides its own special kind of amusement. Like her plays and films, it leads, if not to a proper ending, to a pleasurable continuance.

A great many stills and illustrations from the last six decades can be found in this book. They tell a tale all their own. There are, however, few pictures of Mae from her extreme youth. A flood in the early thirties destroyed all that she had, save the baby photos reproduced in her autobiography. Because her films were corporate enterprises, where I have felt it necessary, I have included illustrations of important scenes or personalities associated with her film work in which she does not appear. This is only fair to the performers who helped make those films successful.

What has concerned me most is factual accuracy in dealing with her theatrical and cinematic appearances. Nowhere else can this material be found in a single place. Popularity in the entertainment industry is a matter of merchandising, promotion, talent, and, ultimately, a genius for dollars and cents. You cannot separate business from it, because business is fundamental to it. Perhaps Miss West summarized it aptly when she commented that at a very tender age she learned two and two make four and five will get you ten, if you work it right.

Naturally, there are pros and cons about writing a book about the career of a person who is still active. The reader might feel an author is constrained by various considerations of a personal nature from telling everything he knows or in his critical evaluations. Because of the fashion in which I have limited my subject, I hope this will not be said of my book. Facts concern me far more than opinions. The facts, I trust, the reader will weigh according to their worth; my opinions he can take or leave, as suits his temperament or inclination.

Without the kind assistance of many friends in the motion picture industry, this book could never have been written. Especially helpful have been the staff and management of MCA-Universal, which owns world rights to nine of Miss West's eleven feature films. In recognition of this kindness, and thinking the reader may wish to view her pictures himself, I have seen fit to include rental and contact information to make nontheatrical bookings more convenient. It is one of the wonders of our age that, at will, on a giant screen in our own homes we have access to the riches of the finest form of entertainment men have yet devised.

Mae West with Libby Taylor, her maid, in her Hollywood apartment, 1934

What I term a cinematograph is a critical method for dealing with a film. There are eleven of these in this book. The format of a cinematograph is to give title and release information, technical credits, casts with character identifications, and then a report on current negative and printing facilities, availability, and other legal data. What follows is the body, specifying the contributing factors, the state of the industry at the time, background and biographical information on the personnel, a plot synopsis, concluding with an appraisal of the film's effect upon initial release and its importance today.

The cinematographs on Mae's films from *Night After Night* through *Klondike Annie* were originally published in somewhat different form in *Views & Reviews* magazine. I had copies of them sent to Miss West and asked her to check them. It had been my intention to confine myself to just these six films. Then something happened, surprising to me but probably not to Miss West. Editors from several cinema magazines here and abroad contacted me asking to include one or another cinematograph in their respective publications. I was at work on other pressing matters and didn't wish to expend the effort. I later wrote to The Citadel Press and proposed bringing out a volume on her films. They agreed to publish it, but suggested I also cover the noncinematic aspects of her career, particularly her stage work. I certainly do not regret having done so. In many ways, her material for the stage surpasses her films in brilliance. Her plays and stories, *The Constant Sinner* among them, reveal a stylistic command of literary technique both rare and unusual, if undeservedly neglected. I thought it best, with one exception, to publish no more of this material prior to its issuance here.

As powerful an impetus as the current enthusiasm for what is called nostalgia has given the publishing industry, I must confess I have found many of the books on cinematic and theatrical history disappointing. They appear to be chiefly compilations of publicity stills with little or no text. Moreover, such books are frequently prone to massive exaggerations or misstatements. To treat of Miss West in this fashion would be singularly unjust in light of her significant contribution. In order to satisfy my objectives in this book, and give the reader something of substance for his money, I have delved back not only into the trades but into studio files for my information. Karl Thiede, research editor for *Views & Reviews*, has proven invaluable to me in this respect along with countless people in the industry familiar with Miss West or who have availed me of closely held data. Miss West's autobiography, to which I have already referred, because of its penchant for authenticity, is an outstanding document of its kind and has been pressed into service, where needed. In my effort to confirm everything by corroboration from more than one source, I was astonished at its truthfulness.

I would not wish to predict what effect, if any, this book will have on how cinema history is *written* in the future. It is a relatively new discipline and is presently in the throes of severe growing pains. I have declared what my intentions have been. It is for you, the reader, to judge by how far I may have missed the mark.

The Early Theatrical Career

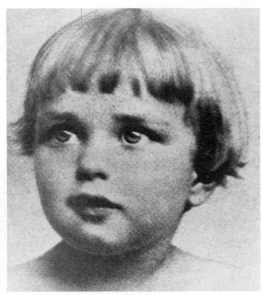

Mae West in a rare baby photo

Mae, about 1908

Mae West was born on 17 August 1893 in Brooklyn. Her father, John West, had been a prizefighter when he married Matilda Delker Doelger, Mae's mother. Encouraged by his wife to find some other vocation, he turned first to a livery stable business, later became a private detective, and finally went into real estate. When Mae was five, her sister, Beverly, was born, and her brother John Edwin followed the next year.

"I was different from my sister and brother," Mae told Ruth Biery for a life story article in four parts beginning in January, 1934, in *Movie Classic*. "My mother had to use the strap or show it to 'em to make 'em mind. But if she gave me an unkind word, I would sulk for days. I was sulky and stubborn. And my mother insisted upon my having my own way. 'Let her go; she's different,' my mother would tell my father."

Her mother took her to vaudeville shows. At five Mae was giving imitations of Bert Williams and Eddie Foy at church socials. Enrolled at seven in "Professor" Watts' Dancing School, she made her debut at the Royal Theatre on Fulton Street, Brooklyn, in one of his regular concerts, doing a song and dance number with a twelve-piece orchestra. Amateur night appearances followed. She played child parts with stock companies until she was eleven, working for Hal Clarendon in New York and on the road in shows like *Little Nell*, *The Marchioness*, and *Mrs. Wiggs of the Cabbage Patch*.

When Mae turned fifteen, she went on the vaudeville stage as a bonneted girlfriend working with William Hogan, an actor who did a Huckleberry Finn characterization. Frank Wallace, a song and dance man with a jazz style and good looks, was on the same bill. Mae at seventeen teamed up with him and they went on the road with their act. On 11 April 1911 they were married at Milwaukee, Wisconsin.

Mae's first real break came with the legitimate show *A la Broadway* which opened 22 September 1911 at the Folies-Bergere Theatre, New York. It ran for eight performances as the bottom half of a double bill topped by *Hello, Paris*, which, in a different form, had first opened there solo on 19 August and ran for thirty performances before the merger. The Folies-Bergere was a theatre-restaurant managed by Henry B. Harris and Jesse L. Lasky. Lasky later became an executive with Paramount, as did William LeBaron, whose book and lyrics served as the basis for *A la Broadway*. *Variety* reviewed the cabaret show on 16 September 1911 while *A la Broadway* was still in rehearsal for an out-of-town opening. By 30 September, *Variety* reported the novelty theatre's closing due to limited seating capacity and past losses totaling $100,000. Mae got good reviews. She quotes several of them in her autobiography. *The New York Times* commented: "Again there was some color and pretty movement in a Continental march by the chorus, and a girl named Mae West, hitherto unknown, pleased by her grotesquerie and a snappy way of singing and dancing."

A LA BROADWAY

Book by William LeBaron. Music by Harold Orlob. Lyrics by William LeBaron and M.H. Hollins.

CAST (without character identifications):

James Bradbury	Octavia Broske
Will Phillips	Mae West
Agostino Vaci	Harriet Leidy
James Cook	Emily Monte
John Lorenz	Virginia Gunther
Ted Westus	Betty Scott
Margaret Taylor	Pat Neaves
Wallace Nedringhaus	Miriam Sanford
Ernest Collins	Martha Edmunds
Ida Harris	Gladys Turner
Glenn Eastman	Florence Warner
Kitty Kyle	

Mae's next venture was for the Shuberts in their Winter Garden revue which opened out of town. Mae was stricken with a cold. *Variety* reported on 25 November 1911 that "she is expected back in the show as soon as possible." The revue was called *Vera Violetta*, two hours of musical comedy based on an hour-long German original, in which Al Jolson proved the big hit. Reviews in the New York papers were mixed and much was revised by the time Mae rejoined the cast. The show ran for 112 performances, opening at the Winter Garden on 20 November 1911. Due to her illness, Mae was not present on reviewer's night. Performances were always computed in terms of six a week, with two matinees on Wednesday and Saturday, averaging eight a week in a typical run.

VERA VIOLETTA

Musical Entertainment in Two Scenes by Leonard Liebling and Harold Attridge from the German of Leo Stein. Music by Edmund Eysler.

CAST (without character identifications):

Edward Cutter	Melville Ellis
Al Jolson	Gaby Deslys
Doris Cameron	Stella Mayhew
Van Rensselaer Wheeler	The Gordon Brothers
James B. Carson	Harry Fisher
Mae West	Clarence Harvey
Barney Bernard	Maidie Berker
Billie Taylor	Jane Lawrence
Florence Douglas	Lew Quinn
Jose Collins	Mel Ryder

On 11 April 1912, *A Winsome Widow* opened at the Moulin Rouge, the new name for the old New York Theatre. It was presented by Florenz Ziegfeld, Jr., and produced by Klaw and Erlanger, who had just closed *The Man From Cook's*. Based on the Charles H. Hoyt play *A Trip to Chinatown*, songs and music were added. Harry Conor returned in his original role as Welland Strong. Even though the revue needed considerable editing, the New York press responded positively. The *New York World* wrote: "It is in every sense a tip-top show, and all the better because at the height of hilarity it is never marred by unpleasant suggestiveness."

Leon Errol, later known for his comedy shorts in Hollywood, did a series of dance numbers. Charles King, who played in *Broadway*

1911

1911

Melody (MGM, 1930), appeared with Elizabeth Brice, of Brice and King at the time, in song and dance sequences. *Variety* said of Mae on 20 April 1912: "The remainder of the music made no impression, excepting 'Piccolo,' a pretty melody, spoiled in the singing by Mae West, a rough soubret, who did a 'Turkey' just a bit too coarse for this $2.00 audience." The show ran for 172 performances.

A WINSOME WIDOW

COMEDY WITH MUSIC IN THREE ACTS. BASED ON "A TRIP TO CHINATOWN" BY CHARLES H. HOYT. MUSIC BY RAYMOND HUBBELL.

CAST

Mrs. Gadder   Fawn Conway
Mrs. Noyes   Katherine Smythe
Mrs. Howell   Lottie Vernon
Mrs. Flippant   Marie Baxter
Flirt   Ethel Kelley
Slaven   Harry Kelley
Rashleigh Gay   Charles J. Ross
Wilder Daly   Charles King
Ben Gay   Leon Errol
Tony   Ida Adams
Isabel   Elizabeth Brice
Mrs. Duer   Natalie Dagwell
Mrs. Guyer   Emmy Wehlen
Willie Grow   Kathleen Clifford
Welland Strong   Harry Conor
Noah   Frank Tinney
Bryton Farley   Sidney Jarvis
Rosie and Jenny   Dolly Twins
La Petite Daffy   Mae West
Mons. McGinnis   Jack Clifford
Mlle Bridie   Irene Weston
Owner of Cliff House   Charles Mitchell
Chief of Police   A. Brannigan
Officer O'Mara   J. McDermott
Mlle. Nana   By Herself
Mons. Alexis   By Alexis
with Fancy Skaters, Cathleen Pope, and George Kirnen.

(Note: Casts are given as published in the trades, the Billboard Index, *and actual theatre programs. The same practice is used throughout Mae's later starring vehicles.)*

Following **Winsome Widow**, Mae concentrated on developing for herself a successful vaudeville act with which she could go on tour. She appeared, among other engagements, at New York's Fifth Avenue Theatre as one of ten acts on the bill for the week of 3 October 1913. She limited the singing content and tried comic monologue, with encouraging success.

She wrote an original eighteen-minute sketch for herself and Beverly, who was now also attempting to break into vaudeville. The act was variously billed as "Mae West and Sister" and "Mae West and Beverly." On 18 November 1913, *Variety* gave her a scathing review: "Mae West in big time vaudeville may only be admired for her persistency in believing she is a big time act and trying to make vaudeville accept her as such. . . . 'Sister's' hair looks very much like Mae's, and there the family resemblance ceases in looks as well as work, for 'Sister' isn't quite as rough as Mae West can't help but being. Unless Miss West can tone down her stage presence in every way she just as might well hop right out of vaudeville into burlesque. . . . The

Mae, the rising vaudeville star

act did very well at the Fifth Avenue Tuesday afternoon. . . . Mae responded to the applause with a speech. She said: 'I am very pleased, ladies and gentlemen, you like my new act. It's the first time I have appeared with my sister. They all like her, especially the boys who always fall for her, but that's where I come in—I always take them away from her.' '' In her autobiography Mae remarks, "We never did much of a sister act. I always liked to go it alone."

There is no room in the conception of the Mae West character for modesty, failure, or prolonged struggle, so there isn't much about these things in what she has written of her early career. They were there all the same, always met with confidence in the vaudeville years, but her life was not without its setbacks. Her marriage to Frank Wallace did not work out, but she didn't divorce him at once, which was to prove costly.

In August 1915, it was announced that Mae West had signed a contract with Universal Pictures, and she went to the West Coast for four weeks. Apparently nothing came of it. She did appear briefly in the farce *Such Is Life* in San Francisco.

Mae continued her activity in vaudeville. In 1916 she was on the bill for a week at Hammerstein's Theatre. "Mae West now has a red carpet rolled out," *Variety* said on 7 July 1916. "She loses much by occasionally overstepping the line between facetiousness and freshness. When she learns to draw the line she will have made a marked stride in the right direction."

She teamed up for a time with Bobby O'Neil and Harry Laughlin, renaming them "the Girard Brothers," because, in her words, "it had class." Frank Bohm, an agent, and Chris Brown, a vaudeville circuit booker, liked the act and it went on tour. Mae introduced a suggestive wiggle into her performance that got the act "fired" in New Haven and Mae in trouble with the theatre manager and the local newspapers. Audiences, principally young males, were delighted and cheered her most places she played.

Frank Bohm was enthusiastic. He guaranteed her $350 a week to do a single and $750 a week as a headliner. He advised her to dispense with the Girard Brothers. She did. She bought expensive clothing and decked herself with stylish gowns. One of them cost $540, was slit up the thigh, clinging to her skin; she sparkled with diamonds. Her tour proved extremely successful.

Mae later recalled for Malcolm H. Oettinger in the September, 1933, issue of *Picture Play*: "I was in Chi at the time, doin' vaudeville, a single. And after the show one night I goes to this jernt where spades have a cabaret, see? And I see them dancing the bump and the jelly roll and all them, then a girl starts doin' a funny sort of dance and I asks, 'What's that?' and the waiter says, 'Oh, lady, that's shakin' the shimmy.' Next night I put it into my act and it like to tore the house down. That audience went wild over it. I took ten bows. The manager come backstage and wanted to know what caused the riot. When I showed him, he was afraid to let me do it again. But next week in Milwaukee they loved it."

On 4 October 1913 Mae West took another step upward. She opened as a headliner in New York at the Shubert Theatre in a two-act musical play, *Sometime*, presented by Arthur Hammerstein with Ed Wynn; the latter also had a substantial role. New York got its

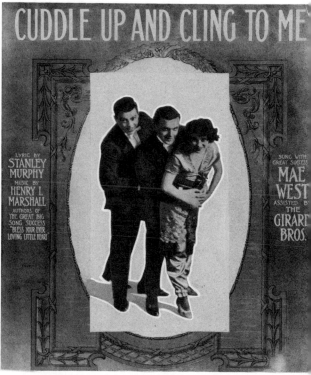

Posing with the Girard Brothers on a sheet music cover

The beginning of the sultry Mae West look

A daring vamp pose

introduction to the shimmy with this play, which prompted a comment made ten years later in the *Variety* of 1 August 1928, remembering Mae West in **Sometime**: "It's not what you can do, but the way you do it that counts." In her autobiography, Mae suggested that this might be fitting as her epitaph. The show ran for 283 performances.

The shimmy came near the end of the show. On 6 October 1918 the *New York Herald Tribune* wrote, "Mae West gave a capital characterization of a chorus girl in search of temptation, but never finding it, which toward the close of the show was marred by vulgarity." *Billboard* on 18 October commented on the novel use in the play of motion picture techniques like the cutback and the close-up. The reviewer thought Ed Wynn "funny and frequent." He added, "Mae West, a pretty young girl of attractive personality, gave a fine performance of a vampire lady, exhibiting a delightful talent for comic art. Her song, 'Any Kind of Man,' was received by the audience with well deserved enthusiasm."

Variety on 11 October 1918 was scalding: "Miss West . . . did her dance known in the dumps as 'The Shimmy Shawabble,' and coming under the heading technically for the better houses of a cooch above the waist. . . . But Miss West, with the assistance of what sounded like a well-placed claque, stopped the show with it, then made a speech, and then made another. . . . Miss West has improved somewhat in looks but is still the rough hand-on-the-hip character portrayer that she first conceived as the ideal type of a woman single in vaudeville." The first act was summed up as having too much of everything, "but in particular Ed Wynn."

Choruses were added to Mae's first song, "All I Want Is Just a Little Lovin'," as encores. The show closed in July, 1919. It was her first substantial theatrical New York success.

SOMETIME

MUSICAL ROMANCE IN TWO ACTS. BOOK AND LYRICS BY RIDA JOHNSON YOUNG. MUSIC BY RUDOLF FRIML. STAGED BY OSCAR EAGLE. DANCES ARRANGED BY ALLAN FOSTER.

CAST:

Mame Dean   Mae West
Henry Vaughan   Harrison Brockbank
Phyllis   Beatrice Summers
Loney Bright   Ed Wynn
Enid Vaughan   Francine Larrimore
Dressing room girls   Betty Stivers, Virginia Lee
Joe Allegretti   Charles DeHaven
Mike Mazetti   Fred Nice
Richard Carter   John Merkyl
Sylvia DeForrest   Frances Cameron
Argentine dancer   Mildred LeGue
Argentine singer   William Dorrian
Apthorp   Albert Sackett
George Gray   Harold Williams
Roof garden manager   Francis Murphy
Mr. Jones   George Gaston

Shortly before **Sometime,** Mae met her mother's attorney, James Timony, who was also a promoter. He was infatuated with her and, increasingly, assisted and advised her professionally. When **Sometime** went on tour, Mae chose to stay in New York and reentered vaudeville with a sixteen-minute musical act incorporating the shimmy. *Variety* reviewed the act 19 September 1919, the week it played the Fifth Avenue, finding the dance "a bit broad for vaudeville," but went on to comment that "Miss West was an unqualified hit. . . ." "Two costumes are worn," the reviewer added, "the first a black and white combination, very tasteful, and the second a silver jet, that looks like a million dollars. . . . Miss West shows a marked improvement in method and delivery. . . ."

The Capitol Theatre, upon its opening, staged an extravagant entertainment befitting New York's most sumptuous amusement palace. Ned Wayburn put on a three-hour **Demi Tasse Revue** consisting of ten elaborate musical and comedy acts. The performance was followed at 11:00 P.M. by the screening of United Artists' first release, **His Majesty, the American**, starring Douglas Fairbanks, Sr. Mae West was included with her sixteen-minute vaudeville act in slightly revised form, singing an Indian ditty, "Laughing Water," and doing the shimmy during her second number, "Oh, What a Moanin' Man," with Arthur Franklin as her accompanist.

Mae continued to secure excellent bookings for her shimmy act, opening with the Winter Garden show in November 1919. It was now that she began to write a whole series of sketches, comic and musical, that required only piano accompaniment. Repeated exposure to audiences helped her perfect a natural gift.

The Mimic World of 1921, shortened to just *The Mimic World* by most references, was a sad bomb that opened at the Century Promenade on 15 August 1921 and closed on 10 September after only twenty-seven performances. Despite the fact that J. J. Shubert directed it personally, the best thing *Billboard* could say of the revue was, "The Century Promenade has seen some pretty bad shows, but *The Mimic World of 1921* is the very peak of worthlessness." The review also said, "Yes, Miss West certainly wiggled. And Wiggled. AND WIGGLED." Presumably Mae got herself up for the finale as Our Lady of Fatima during an appearance, and in this setting did her shimmy. *Variety* commented on 26 August 1921: "In a tent it would have been a riot."

THE MIMIC WORLD OF 1921

A Revue in Two Acts With Lines and Lyrics by Harold Atteridge, James Hussey, and Owen Murphy. Music by Jean Swartz, Lew Pollack, and Owen Murphy. Directed by J.J. Shubert. Staged by Allan K. Foster.

CAST: Act I, Scene 1—At the Club

Tom   Lou Edwards
Dick   Eddie Hickey
Harry   Albert Wiser
John   Clarence Harvey
Howard Dashing   Frank Hurst

Act I, Scene 2—Times Square at Midnight
Cliff   Cliff Edwards
Officer   Eddie Hickey
Blind Man   Frank Masters
Anti Volstead   Lou Edwards
Yonson   El Brendel
Evelyn   Evelyn Martyn
James Bradstreet   Albert Wiser
A Card Shark   William Moran
Gunman   Lou Edwards

In the revue *The Mimic World* (1921)

Shifty Liz Mae West
Salvation Army Officer Frank Masters

Act I, Scene 3—Broadway Pirates

Captain Kidd Up-to-date Gladys James
His First Mate Peggy Brown
    and the Twentieth Century Pirates

Act I, Scene 4—An Elopement

Yonson El Brendel
Hilda Swanson Flo Burt

Act I, Scene 5—Cafe de Paris

Phil William Moran
Louis Albert Wiser
An Entertainer Frank Masters
Miss Promenade Gladys James
Madelon Mae West

Act I, Scene 6—A Few Moments With

Ukelele Ike Cliff Edwards

Act I, Scene 7—A Hat Store

Hats Moran and Wiser
Lieutenant Black Eddie Hickey
Miss Shopping Ann Toddings

Act I, Scene 8—On the Street

Mailman Frank Masters
Maid Peggy Brown

Act I, Scene 9—Merry Mixups

The Conversationalists Bard and Pearl

Act I, Scene 10—Shakespeare's Garden of Love

A Page Ann Toddings
Shakespeare Frank Hurst
Hamlet Lou Edwards
Ophelia Helen Neidova
Romeo C.L. Henderson
Juliet Madeline Smith
Othello Cliff Edwards
Desdemona Marjorie Carville
Portia Flo Burt
Bassanio Eddie Hickey
Anthony Albert Wiser
Cleopatra Mae West
Petruchio Frank Masters
Katherine Elizabeth Morgan
Richard III Clarence Harvey
Queen Anne Gladys James
Henry VIII William Moran

Act II
Scene 1   Tennis Terpsichorean
Scene 2   Jazzimova
Scene 3   In Yonson's Drawing Room
Scene 4   At the Studio
Scene 5   Temptation
Scene 6   At the Museum
Scene 7   An Interlude with Mae West
Scene 8   A Girl's Fancy
Scene 9   In Yonson's Kitchen
Scene 10   At the Opera
Scene 11   At the Fight

From *The Mimic World*

Left: Posing during first World War days

A candid shot from the mid-twenties

Jack Dempsey, then World's Heavyweight Champion, and his manager, Jack Kearns, attended the premiere of **Mimic World**. After the show, they came backstage to Mae's dressing room. Dempsey wanted her to do a Pathé picture with him, probably a serial, to be titled **Daredevil Jack**. Kearns proposed that Mae do a screen test with Dempsey and they go on the Pantages Circuit cross-country, winding up in Hollywood, where they could star in the film. Mae did make the screen test, a love scene, but Timony dissuaded her from going on tour. The Pantages Circuit required three performances a day, which was too taxing. So Mae got up a new act with Harry Richman. Dempsey went on circuit, but he didn't make the picture.

Mae's interest in the subject of sexuality and in its dramatic potential for the stage began to consume her. She recognized that an entire side of reality had escaped artistic expression. She took, over the next few years, to reading Freud, Jung, Adler, and Havelock Ellis. She wanted to learn everything there was to know about human eroticism. And she wanted to write a full-length stage play incorporating her findings. Timony was excited and agreed to back the project.

In her own published account of her life, Mae has credited Harry Richman generously for his contribution to her vaudeville act. When they appeared together at the Riverside, *Variety* on 23 June 1922 reported: "Mae West, once known to vaudeville fans as a girl who shook a wicked shoulder, will prove a revelation to her former acquaintances in her new act. She rises to heights undreamed of for her and reveals unsuspected depths as a delineator of character songs, a dramatic reader of ability, and a girl with a flare for farce that will some day land her on the legitimate Olympus. In her new turn she is assisted by Harry Richman, who is an ideal opposite. . . . Miss West has arrived and is a real wow. Opening after intermission here, she and her partner did twenty minutes of sheer entertainment that was honey to the jaded vaudeville palate and were then ovated to a speech."

The West-Richman team got quality bookings. Then on 8 September 1922 *Variety* announced that Harry Richman had left Mae to go with Nora Bayes's show. It was scheduled to play the nightclub circuit. Her new freedom from continuous work permitted Mae the opportunity to gain firsthand knowledge of the impact of sex on people. Anyone who reads Mae's **The Constant Sinner** will readily concede that the author was intimately informed on her subject. It tells of life in the dives, among prostitutes, the whole of predatory society. **Sex** would be the first of Mae's popular essays in carnal existence.

I do not know if Mae ever appeared in burlesque. In the twenties, New York had two major circuits—the Mutual, which played the Star Theatre in Brooklyn, and the Columbia, which played the Columbia Theatre. According to the *Billboard* Index, a performer spelling her name "May West" appeared in **Playmates** on the Mutual Circuit the week of 2 October 1922; she played the same circuit in **Girls From the Follies** the week of 5 March 1923. For the week of 31 December 1923, a chorus girl named "Mae West" appeared in **'Round the Town** for Mutual. "May West" was in Mutual's **French Models** for the week of 4 February 1924 and worked the week of 24 November 1924 on the Columbia Circuit in **Lena Daly and Her Miss Tabasco Company**. The week of 9 March 1925 found "May West" in **Snap It Up**. Gene Ringgold for an article in *Screen Facts* (Vol. 2, No. 1), claims "the following year she returned to burlesque in another Wayburn revue," meaning **Demi Tasse**. The Wayburn show wasn't burlesque, but if Mae was "returning" to it, perhaps she did occasionally appear there during her early years. Whatever the truth, Mae didn't learn about sexual mores from books.

Mae's smash hit **Sex**, opened at Daly's Theatre in New York on 26 April 1926 and ran 385 performances. Had it not been raided and had Mae not been jailed, it probably would have run longer. The play closed 19 March 1927 because grosses fell below $7,000 a week, which was the minimum amount required to keep it going. *Variety*, extremely conservative, said on 23 March 1927 that "a dirty play" was "closed by [the] public, any theatre's best censor."

The plot concerned Margie LaMont, a Montreal prostitute, who shares rooms with a blackmailer. The blackmailer induces a New York society woman to visit him in his rooms. Margie finds the woman drugged. She restores her to consciousness. The woman, to hide her shame, accuses Margie of having robbed her. To get even, Margie later seduces and threatens to marry the society woman's only son in New York. At the end, she returns to her favorite naval lieutenant.

Sex opened out of town in New London, Connecticut. Edward Elsner, the director, had a splendid theatrical record of top plays to his credit and had worked with the Barrymores. Daly's Theatre, uptown New York on 63rd Street, was the only one available near Broadway. James Timony was coproducer with C. W. Morganstern, but this fact didn't come out until the trial. Reviewers sought initially to ignore the show. *Billboard* on 8 May 1926 laconically remarked: "The piece is not just low entertainment. It is not entertainment at all. Poorly written, poorly acted, horribly staged, **Sex** does not even contain anything for dirt seekers. The theme is trite and the lines are dull, while the action is simply disgusting."

Mae was cited as having written the play under the *nom de plume* Jane Mast by *The New York Times* on 1 May 1926, adding, "a crude inept play, cheaply produced and poorly acted." *Variety* took an early stand against it on 28 April 1926: "Mae West . . . has broken the fetters and does as she pleases here. After three hours of this play's nasty, infantile, amateurish, and vicious dialog, after watching its various actors do their stuff badly, one really has a feeling of gratefulness for any repression that may have toned down her vaudeville songs in the past. If this show could do one week of good business it would depart with a handsome profit, it's that cheaply put on." The 385 performances were with seats at $3.30. According to Mae, orchestra seats were $10.00.

Sex was one of three plays raided by police on 21 February 1927. Mae West, principal cast members, Edward Elsner, James Timony, and Clarence William Morganstern were arrested and charged with corrupting the morals of youth. Charges against **The Captive** were dropped at the same time; those against **The Virgin Man** were heard in special session. On 20 March 1927 *Variety* carried the names of the **Sex** jurors, their addresses, and occupations. The **Sex** attorney pleaded not guilty. Norman Schloss was the chief counsel for the defense. Charges against John Cort, owner of Daly's, were later dismissed. On 6 April 1927 *Variety* reported that the jurors were out five and one half hours, returning a verdict of guilty. On 20 April 1927 Judge George L.

When her play *Sex* opened on Broadway

"Sex" Wins High Mark For Depravity, Dullness

Audience at Daly's Sits in Dulled Silence During Exhibition of Frankness

"Sex," by Jane Mast, presented by C. William Morganstern at Daly's, with the following cast:

Margie La Mont................Mae West
Lieutenant Gregg, R. N....Harry O'Neill
Rocky Waldron..........Warren Sterling
Agnes Scott.................Ann Reader
Clara Smith.............Eeda von Beulow
Jimmy Stanton........Lyons Wickland
Robert Stanton.............Pacle Ripple
Dawson ....Gordon Burby
Ensign Jones, U. S. N....D. J. Hamilton
Curley ....Al Regalia
Marie ....Constance Morganstern
Jenkins ....Frank Howard
Captain Carter.............George Rogers
Waiter....................Gordon Earle
Red ....Marie Morrisey
Condez ....Conde Brewer
Spanish Dancer.........Michael Markham

During the latter part of its second act, "Sex," which was produced last night at Daly's took on a certain form of drama, not very well-constructed nor well-written drama but yet drama of sorts. Up to that time the play had been an ostensible reflection of the underworld as it is supposed to exist in Montreal and Trinidad. A world of ruthless, evil-minded, foul-mouthed crooks, harlots, procurers and other degenerate members of that particular zone of society.

Never in a long experience of theater going have we met with a set of characters so depraved—and so dull. At the more daring scenes and the more suggestive lines certain members of the audience indulged in laughter as rancous as the performance on the stage; a few sought relief in flight, but the great majority remained in a state of stunned silence, wondering, no doubt, what was to be the next exhibition of complete frankness. All the barriers of conventional word and act that the last few seasons of the theater have left us were swept away and we were shown not sex but lust—stark, naked lust.

The scene of the second act was a cabaret at a cafe in Trinidad, and, with the assistance of a jazz band, it was played with much spirit and abandon. Miss MaMy West, the featured member of the company, contributed a song and dance which, while in no way reducing the temperature of the tropical scene, in our opinion, added but little to the art of the entertainment. Apart from this episode Miss West played the role of Margie La Mont, the principal scarlet lady of the piece, with sincerity if without distinction. The other members of the long cast ranged from fair to very bad.

C. B. D.

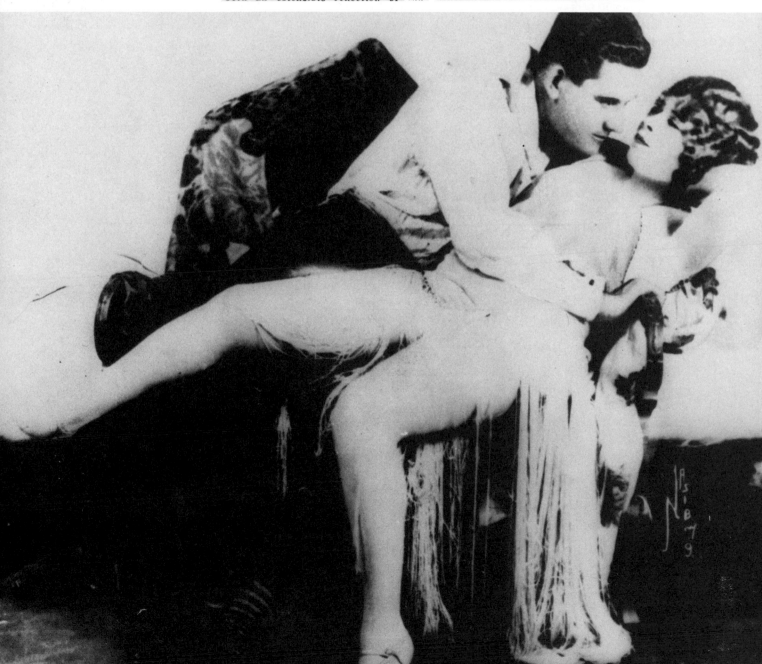

Donelian passed sentence. Mae and Timony both were fined $500 and committed to the workhouse for ten days. Morganstern drew only the prison sentence. The others, by recommendation of New York District Attorney Joab H. Banton, were given suspended sentences. Mae was sent to Welfare Island, where she was released after eight days, for good behavior.

SEX

A COMEDY DRAMA IN THREE ACTS BY JANE MAST (MAE WEST). PRODUCED BY C. WILLIAM MORGANSTERN. STAGED BY EDWARD ELSNER.

CAST

Margie LaMont Mae West
Lieutenant Gregg Barry O'Neill
Rocky Waldron Warren Sterling
Agnes Scott Ann Reader
Clara Smith Edda Von Beulow
Jimmy Stanton Lyons Wickland
Robert Stanton Pacie Ripple
Dawson Gordon Burby
Jones D.J. Hamilton
Curley Al Rigali
Marie Constance Morganstern
Jenkins Frank Howard
Captain Carter George Rogers
Walter Gordon Earle
Red Mary Morrisey
Condex Conde Brewer
Spanish dancers Michael Markham,
        Fred LeQuorne, Florence Doherty
Flossie Ida Mantell
Waiter Frank R. Wood
The Fleet Band The Syncopators
Featuring the Fleet Orchestra directed by Joe Candullo

(Note: This cast listing is as of 26 April 1926. Florence Doherty was added to the cast in early May, 1926, and so has been interpolated. Ethel Mantell was added to the cast and deleted in June, 1926. Dave Hughes replaced Al Rigali briefly in May, 1926, with Rigali returning in June, 1926. Edward Kirby replaced Frank Howard in May, 1926. Pete Segreto was added to the cast as a sailor in August, 1926. Albert Benald replaced D.J. Hamilton as Ensign Jones in September, 1926, with Hamilton resuming his role in December, 1926, Benald leaving. Irving Jardin replaced Fred LeQuorne as a Spanish Dancer in October, 1926 until LeQuorne returned to the cast in January, 1927.)

Prior to the raid on *Sex,* Mae had written another play which dealt confidentially and frankly with the subject of male homosexuality. It was called *The Drag* and again credited the pseudonymous Jane Mast with its authorship. *"The Drag* treated seriously the problems of a homosexual," Mae has written, "and showed how his abnormal tendencies brought disaster to his family, his friends, and himself. It stated that an intelligent understanding of the problems of all homosexuals by society could avert such social tragedies."

The Drag opened at Poll's Park Theatre at Bridgeport, Connecticut, on a tryout before Broadway on 31 January 1927. While Mae had no role, C. W. Morganstern was the producer. The play was subtitled "a homosexual comedy drama in three acts." James Timony was also an investor; Edward Elsner directed. There were some forty

With Lyons Wickland in *Sex*

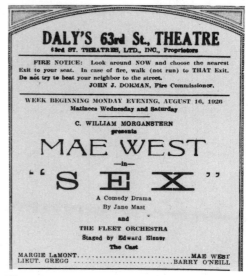

The program of *Sex*

In a "daring" scene from the play *Sex,* with Warren Sterling

33

Mae West in Court After "Sex" Raid

(The crisis in Mae West's career came with "Sex," the frank, lurid drama which aroused the attention of the British Embassy and provoked police to raid the show. Read how the current triumphant, smiling sinner of the screen passed through a prison ordeal and carried her idea through to success.)

CHAPTER V.

By MARTIN SOMMERS.

(Copyright: 1933; by News Syndicate Co., Inc.)

THE funniest story told about that exciting Night Court scene on Feb. 9, 1927,

tence on April 19, 1927, Timoney and Morganstern went to the Tombs for ten days each.

Mae's play, "The Drag," dealing with events at a Broadway fairyland party, didn't open on Broadway, after Paterson, N. J., tryouts. One report was that official New York saw the drama at a very secret and private showing, after which thumbs were turned down on it. Mae's own story was that she withheld it from Broadway presentation at the time because the public was "too child-like to face like grownups the problem of homosexuality."

When she left Welfare Island, it was Warden Schleth himself who pronounced Mae "a fine woman—a great character."

Unbeaten, the actress went on to her greatest Broadway triumph on the legitimate stage, "Diamond Lil," a play which had Park Avenue as well as the wisenheimers of the Main Stem at her feet. It was a great, bawdy, rollicking production, full of salt and malt. Sometimes real beer flowed from the taps of "Suicide Hall," for the laughing evil-doers on the stage—

the wisecracking, rough-and-tumble members of the cast. Mae, looking like a brewery calendar beauty, swaggered across the stage victorious. We'll hear about how she over-ate to play "Diamond Lil" tomorrow.

Follow Mr. Sommers' backstage life story of Mae West in tomorrow's Pink and other editions of The News.

Hot Grenades From West-ern Front

Sommers: Don't you think they'll be an epidemic of smiling sinners who triumph to the end in the movies now?

Miss West: Copy my stuff? Say, they can put all the scarlet women they like on the screen, and all the tenderloin stories. It's my clowning they can't copy and it's the laughs that make me different.

buttons. Find them yourself. Who do you think I am—your wife?"

The film censors today have approved hotter, wickeder lines.

But Mae changed her silk stockings for cotton and went to Welfare Island prison because of "Sex," when Judge George E. Donnellan gave her a ten-day sen-

---

Welfare Island Fails to Tame The Wild West

Top—The cast and producers of "Sex," in General Sessions in March, 1927. 1—C. W. Morgenstern, one of owners, 2—Robert Burney, attorney, 3—Mae West. 4—Barry P. O'Neal, actor. 5—Pacie Ripple, actress. 6—Florence Doherty, actress. 7—Mary Morrissey, actress. 8—Ann Reeder, actress. 9 — Norman Schloss, attorney. Above—Jack Hughes, Jack Cheatham, Mae West and Joe Skinner (l. to r.) in a scene from "Diamond Lil."

the beer baron now in Sing Sing, helped finance her show, Mae had to fight for "Sex." It had its first try-out in New London. The theatre management there objected to the title. The first night only about 120 customers appeared.

James A. Timoney, one of Mae's backers and her close and faithful friend for years, urged the actress to change the title. So did

when Acting Mayor Joseph V. McKee, then Chief Executive during a James J. Walker absence, led raids on three Broadway shows, was overlooked at the time.

Mae West's "Sex," with Mae as the rough, tough, wicked and impenitent Margie Lamonte, had been wowing 'em on Broadway for almost a year, and Mae was established as a dramatic star. Helen Menken, the sad-faced, intellectual actress, was playing in the extremely highbrow French play, "The Captive," in which Eduard

Bourdet, Parisian playwright, attempted to interpret how woman may prove stronger than the bonds of matrimony. Misses West and Menken, so the story goes, met in a flurry of bondsmen who had stampeded into Night Court. Both raided grand dames of the stage were surrounded by their faithful casts.

"Sex" vs. "The Captive."

Mae was defending her play, famous for a hot second act in which "loose women follow the fleet" to Trinidad, and on this British island sailors carouse in a brothel, with drunken dames reeling about. Informal debate on "Sex" vs. "The Captive" got pretty torrid.

Miss Menken didn't think much of "Sex," Miss West thought even less of "The Captive." After considerable of a squabble, Mae is reported to have gathered her ermines about her and carried the night with the succinct remark:

"Well, anyhow we're normal!"

From the time Owney Madden,

his associate, C. W. Morganstern. John Cort, then 67, and for 50 years active in the theatre, came to New London from Broadway, interested because "Sex" was scheduled to open in Daly's Theatre, which he controlled. He also urged changes in the drama.

They Couldn't Change Her Mind

"They worked on me for hours," Mae says in telling of how she stuck to her "Sex." But they could not change the determined star's mind.

"The second night when I arrived at the theatre a littled discouraged, there were long lines of sailors and Coast Guardsmen waiting to buy tickets," she narrates. "The house was packed that night and every night after.

"Believe me, I'll never forget the Navy. The Navy helped plenty."

The career of "Sex" was stormy throughout. The British Embassy made an investigation of the representation given of the high jinks, strumpeting, and trolloping going on at Trinidad.

Then, after about 700 policemen and seven Assistant District Attorneys had seen the play without apparent injury to their morals during its long and successful run, came the raid. Charges of "corrupting the morals of youth, or others" were preferred against Miss West, Morganstern, Timoney, and nineteen members of the cast. They were found guilty on evidence that doesn't appear very damning today, in the light of the way the public is supporting Mae West, tart triumphant when she rapid-fires her funny lines in "She Done Him Wrong," her hit picture.

One of the lines held objectionable in "Sex" was in a scene between Margie (Mae West), and a vulture named Rocky (Warren Sterling).

Rocky to Margie: "Where's my collar button?"

Margie: "They're your collar

Posing for the press photographers

"gay" people in the cast. *The Captive*, which was raided simultaneously with *Sex,* contained a display of lesbianism, but went nowhere nearly as far as *The Drag*. One-sheets in Bridgeport advertised it as being "more sensational than *Rain* or *Sex*." Opening night was a sell-out and many were turned away.

A *Variety* reviewer gave the play his critique on 2 February 1927. His pretense was that the subject of the play should be dealt with seriously, but that by showing how homosexuals behave with one another, rather than relying on offstage occurrences and indirect descriptions, the "play was a cheap and shabby appeal to sensationalism," and "a jazzed-up revel on the garbage heap." The high point of the play came in the third act, without dialogue or dramatic action. The *Variety* reviewer summarized the drag sequence: "Some thirty young men take part in the spectacle, half tricked out in women's clothes and half in tuxedos. Half a dozen of the boys in skirts do specialities, and the episode takes on the character of a chorus girl 'pickout' number in a burlesque show. . . . All hands are rouged, lip-sticked, and liquid-whited to the last degree. During the whole scene a jazz orchestra plays 'hot' music in the background."

In her autobiography Mae claims to have come out ahead by $30,000 after only a two-week engagement. On 9 February 1927 *Variety* mentioned that Beverly West had been arrested on a disorderly conduct charge in connection with the opening. A private performance of *The Drag* in New York for city officials and twenty-five physicians to garner their endorsement failed. This might, in fact, have precipitated the raid on *Sex*. The success of Gore Vidal's *Myra Breckenridge* more than forty years later indicates how popular the subject still is with audiences.

THE DRAG

A Homosexual Comedy in Three Acts by Jane Mast (Mae West). Staged by Edward Elsner. Produced by C. William Morganstern.

CAST

Dr. Richmond   Elmer Grandin
Barbara Richmond   Emily T. Francis
A Maid   Jane Young
David Caldwell   Allan Campbell
Clem Hathaway   Leo Howe
Judge Kingsbury   A. Francis Lenz
Taxi Driver   Sam Mass
Claire   Margaret Hawkins
Roland Kingsbury   Jay Sheridan
Butler   George Du Vall
Rosco Gillingwater   Charles Townsend
Jack Winifred   Charles Ordway
Hal Swanson   Harry Shlegle
Alan Grayson   Marshall Bradford
Marion Hunter   Marion Davis
Billy   Arthur Rowse
Guests at the drag: Herbert Sullivan, Bobby D'Andrea, Eugene Casali, Allan Gray, Gus Shilling, Ed Hearne, Stuart Callaghan, John Mangum, Harry Carroll, Edi Ellis, Sylvan Repetti, Howard Ditley, Dick Gray, John Rosimer, Frank Carroll, James King, George Du Vall, Fred Dickens, Charles Langston, Jimmy Barry.

The Wicked Age was Mae's next play to open off-Broadway. It had a tryout near the end of September at the Shubert Theatre in New Haven. The *Long Branch Daily Record* found it "gross, disgusting, tiresome, utterly futile vulgarity, without a single excusing feature or reason for being." The *New Haven Journal-Courier* felt it "devoid of any merit." *Variety* was somewhat less outspoken in its review of 28 September 1927. It said that Mae was trying to cash in on the *Sex* sensation, that there were "no names in the cast and no outstanding performances," and that "throughout . . . the audience gave the piece the razz."

Although Anton F. Scibilia, C. W. Morganstern's one-time partner, was credited with being the producer, James Timony's money was also behind it. Superstitious about location, Timothy had *The Wicked Age* open in New York once more at Daly's 63rd Street Theatre on 4 November 1927. It ran all of nineteen performances, closing on 19 November.

The story concerned Babe Carson, in Burns Mantle's description "a plump flapper." Her guardian refuses to let Babe go to a roadhouse, so she brings her intoxicated friends to her home for a necking session. The guardian returns unexpectedly and throws Babe out. She enters and wins a bathing beauty contest. Her name and image are commercially exploited. She is courted by several men.

Raymond Jarno's contract called for him to play the male lead. After the tryout, Mae cut his part. Jarno went to the arbitration board and appealed. Opening night, with a ruling in his favor, everyone had to go back to playing the piece the old way. The cast were unsure of themselves.

Mae got a chance to introduce a lot of witty dialogue. Babe comments in the first act, "While he was a quarterback at Notre Dame, he's now a fullback for this dame."

> *Flapper:* I was up in the Count's room alone last night. Did I do wrong?
> *Babe:* How do I know? Don't you remember?

> *Contest Judge:* I kiss your hand now, Madamoiselle, and later I will kiss you some more.
> *Babe:* Fifty million Frenchmen can't be wrong.

Babe remarks that she has no objection to staging a publicity stunt, riding down Broadway astride a white horse like a contemporary Lady Godiva. It's been years since people saw a horse on Broadway. When a company proposes to run an ad on a condensed milk product, saying "Drink Babe Carson's milk—it never runs dry!", Babe complains that it sounds like she's a cow.

The New York Times reacted: "The whole was in the best Mae West school of playwriting and acting—that of just saying one word after another with no regard for any sort of technique and less for common sense. A cast of some thirty players participated. At least one thing must be said for Miss West—she does give work to a lot of performers who otherwise might be without jobs." *Billboard* commented on 12 November 1927: "It is dull, sluggish, bloated. It is a set of pornographic pictures cleaned up somewhat and brought to life. It drools with a foolish, slobbery grimace."

"*The Wicked Age* is labeled a satirical comedy," *Variety* reported. "Actually, it's a burlesque, with the satire at the expense of an auditor of a mentality above the eighth grade. . . . The biggest complaints should be the Columbia-Mutual burlesque wheels, because Miss West is getting $3.85 with something the wheels don't dare at $1.65."

Walking away from trouble

THE WICKED AGE

A Satirical Comedy in Three Acts by Mae West. Staged by Edward Elsner. Settings executed by Premier Studios. Produced by Anton F. Scibilia.

CAST:

Aunt Elizabeth	Emily Francis
Ruth Carson	Doris Haslett
Peggy McShane	Peggy Doran
Willie Weller	Hassell Brooks
Gloria Carson	Ruth Hunter
Robert Carson	Hal Clarendon
John Ferguson	Francis Reynolds
Warren Hathaway	Carroll Daly
The Count	Robert Bentley
Mrs. Martha Carson	Augusta Perry
Evelyn ("Babe") Carson	Mae West
Bob Miles	David Newell
Al Smalley	Hub White
Tom Hathaway	William Langdon
Jack Stratford	Raymond Jarno
Ray Dempster	Harry W. Williams
George Smith	Harold Leonard
Lou Ginsberg	Harry W. Carter
Gladys Blake	Louise Kirtland
Nell Brown	Ethel Maynard
Norma Faire	Wilva Davis
Polly Acker	Phoebe Otis
Annie Lawrence	Billy LeSuer
Mack Hadden	Hal Findlay
Bert Astor	Arthur Boran
Stephany Joy	Veritza Winter
Chauffeur	Pete Segreto
Jazzbo Williams	Mike Jackson
Henry Lee	Thomas Morris
Jeanette	Georgia Clark
Dick Adams	Harry W. Williams
Henry Arthur	Harold Leonard

Plus bathing girls, vendors, cameramen, and people of the town.

Despite their almost universally negative tone, the reviewers were alike in predicting a long run for *The Wicked Age*. It was Mae West herself who closed it. Jarno's voice couldn't carry in a packed house, but Actors' Equity had ruled he must have the lead. Mae tried to pay him full wages if he would only do it her way until a replacement could be found; the wages would extend for the run of the play. When Jarno insisted on doing it as originally rehearsed, Mae shut down rather than do what she felt a bad job of it.

The reader will have to adjust to Miss West's press during the twenties and thirties. It wasn't good. *Variety* had a super-morality and, later in Hollywood, Mae raised Martin Quigley's ire. Quigley was a devout counter-Reformation Catholic who published the *Motion Picture Herald* and the *Motion Picture Almanac*. He was one of the forces behind the Legion of Decency. In the instance of Mae's films, it is now possible to view with equanimity what once appeared so objectionable. This cannot be done with her plays. Mae West was not a professional playwright of light comedies in the way that W. Somerset Maugham and and Noel Coward were. With the exception of *Diamond Lil* and *The Constant Sinner,* they are not available in script or novel form. Her plays, like her screenplays, were designed as settings to show her

Song sheet from *Diamond Lil*

various talents to good advantage. For the most part they were widely accepted by audiences. Play critics, even more than book reviewers, are a peculiar bunch. Like a great many others, Mae had to satisfy herself with popular endorsement. I would add only the following observation: Had her plays won favor with the critics, there is every reason to believe they would have flopped at the box office.

A stage adaptation of *Rain*, based on Maugham's short story "Miss Thompson," was done by John Colton and Clemence Randolph. Jeanne Eagels played the lead. It earned better than a million dollars in royalties for Maugham and the collaborators. Its tremendous success, and the nature of its theme, inspired Mae to write her best-known and most frequently performed stage vehicle, *Diamond Lil*.

Lil opened at the Royale Theatre in New York on 9 April 1928 and closed on 12 January 1929 after 323 performances. Then it went on tour. Jack and Mark Linder volunteered to produce. Mae gave Mark a credit for suggesting the locale and a featured role. Her sister, under the name Beverly Osborne played Sally. Jack LaRue, who would work for Mae in the future, was cast as Pablo, a part I'm sure he performed brilliantly. Rafaella Ottiano portrayed Russian Rita, a role she would have again in the Paramount feature *She Done Him Wrong* with a shortened screen name.

I will recount the *Diamond Lil* plot at length in connection with the film version, and dispense with it here. The critical reviews were quite good, but some were guarded. "Miss West has a fine and direct way of approaching that subject," *The New York Times* wrote on 10 April 1928, meaning sex, "that is almost Elizabethan. If you can stay in the theatre you are likely to enjoy it."

In her autobiography, Mae tells of how she came to conceive of the character Diamond Lil and, in the revised version, how she has defended her copyright to it in court. *Variety* had a different theory. "There was such a Bowery bimbo," the review of 11 April 1928 said. "The original Lil came from Chicago and became known through having a diamond set in one of her front teeth, among other things. Her sway was in the section known as Chatham Square, the first title of the Lil show." Miss West has made no mention of such a prototype, much less *Chatham Square* as an alternate name for the play.

Billboard on 21 April 1928 wrote of it, "Mae West does a much better job with *Diamond Lil* than she did with her previous offerings, altho this negative praise does not mean that she has anything worth bragging about." Mae quotes Robert Garland, drama critic for the *New York Evening Telegram*. If a few critics didn't agree with him, audiences did. ". . . From now on, she's my favorite actress. . . . From now on, I intend to applaud her from the top lines of my column. . . ." The *Times* conceded, "She is a good actress, is Miss West." John Colton congratulated her. And the public confirmed that Mae West had arrived. "I enjoyed my success with no false humility," Mae has written, "and no coy hiding of my ego under a basket. I had worked very hard since a teenager."

DIAMOND LIL

A DRAMA OF THE UNDERWORLD BY MAE WEST. PERIOD AND LOCALE SUGGESTED BY MARK LINDER. STAGED

Diamond Lil

Diamond Lil relaxes

With Jack La Rue

Chick Clark breaks away from Joliet to see his former sweetheart, Diamond Lil

BY IRA HARDS. SÒNG "DIAMOND LIL" WRITTEN BY ROBERT STERLING. SETTINGS BY AUGUST VIMNERA STUDIOS.

CAST

Diamond Lil   Mae West
Captain Cummings   Curtis Cooksey
Chick Clark   Herbert Duffy
Gus Jordan   J. Merrill Holmes
Dan Flynn   Ernest Anderson
Rita Christinia   Rafaella Ottiano
Jim   Mark Linder
Spider Kane   Jack Cheatham
Pablo Juarez   Jack LaRue
Sally   Beverly Osborne
Isaac Jacobson   Louis Nusbaum
Jimmy Biff   Frank Wallace
Steak McGary   Jo-Jo
Frances   Marion Day
Ragtime Kelly   Pat Whalen
Flo   Helene Vincent
Mary Ryan   Thelma Lawrence
Kitty   Mary Martin
Mike   Joseph A. Barrett
Pete the Duke   Ronald Savery
Bill the Waiter   Jack Howard
Steve the Porter   George O'Donnell
Bessie   Marion Johns
Violet   Mildred Ryder
Polly   Annabell Jaenette
Gloria   Debora Kaye
Frank Kelly   David Hughes
Maggie Murphy   Patsy Klein
Skinny Schultz   Clara Cubitt
Officer Doheney   James F. Kelly
The Bowery Terror   Harold Garry
Members of the Slumming Party: Richard K. Keith, Adah Sherman, Agnes Neilson, Elizabeth Pendleton, George O'Donnell, Evelyn Ortega, and Elizabeth Lowe.

While **Diamond Lil** was still playing New York, Mae's comedy drama **Pleasure Man** opened on a tryout in Bridgeport, Connecticut, and then moved for another to the Bronx Opera House on 17 September 1928. Carl Reed, the producer, had been after Mae to do a play for a long time. Mae was credited as the author in all the publicity, but this was the limit of her direct participation. On 19 September 1928 Jack Conway commented in *Variety*: "It's the queerest show you've ever seen. All the queens are in it." He added, "That West girl knows her box-office, and this one is in right now."

The plot concerns a stud who specializes in making women and then jilting them. In the second act, four women gossip, and four female impersonators do their impression of the same thing. The last scene was in drag, reminiscent of Mae's earlier homosexual play. The queens go through their various numbers on stage while the stud is murdered by the husband of a jilted shill. He was a medical student, the husband presently explains to the police, and didn't mean to tap the stud, only incapacitate his reproductive organ.

A strange reflection belongs here. When I was doing an extended study of the Mascot serials, I screened *The Vanishing Legion* (Mascot, 1931). In it, Edward Hearn plays twelve-year-old Frankie Darro's father. They are frequently separated and reunited throughout the course of numerous chapters, because Hearn is a fugitive. But every

Diamond Lil

With Curtis Cooksey in *Diamond Lil*

Rafaella Ottiano

Between J. Merrill Holmes and Ernest Anderson

The complete *Diamond Lil* company on stage

meeting is characterized by necking sessions a trifle too passionate for ordinary parental sobriety. Mae cast him both in *The Drag* and *Pleasure Man*. He was nearly always an extra in her Paramount films, and appears in *My Little Chickadee*. His career suffered undeservedly. It is not possible to witness his wounded, shocked, distressed countenance and not be moved by the fact that in the United States Mae West's plays initiated a movement toward tolerance, if not sympathy, in treating a once-taboo subject.

The official downtown opening of *Pleasure Man* was at the Biltmore on 1 October 1928. It closed after two and one-half performances. The police raided it after the first performance and a second time in the middle of the Wednesday matinee.

Billboard's review on 13 October 1928, somewhat belated, was unduly vicious in its condemnation, called the play "an abomination." It went on: "*Pleasure Man* is prostitution of the rankest sort, a flagrant attempt to capitalize filth and degeneracy and cash in on the resultant cheap publicity." *The New York Times* stated that "some of the players seemed to glory in their opportunities for exhibitionism." *Variety* ran an editorial on 'Is Show Dirt Box-Office Pay Dirt?'' in their 10 October 1928 issue. It took *Pleasure Man* and two other plays to task.

In the October 1933 number of *Shadoplay* magazine, Mae was interviewed by Rae Bartow. Mae observed that seats for *Pleasure Man* were selling between $70 and $100. Had she pleaded guilty after the raids, she could have escaped without a fine. Mae chose to defend. It cost her $60,000. She won. Mae wrote in her autobiography that today *Pleasure Man* could play Broadway unmolested. "After Tennessee Williams' sexual hullabaloos the audiences are now free to face the lower half of man's aspirations on earth without arrest."

PLEASURE MAN

A COMEDY DRAMA IN TWO ACTS BY MAE WEST. STAGED BY CHARLES EDWARD DAVENPORT. SETTINGS BY LIVINGSTON PLATT. COSTUMES DESIGNED BY DOLLY TREE AND EXECUTED BY BROOKS COSTUME COMPANY. PRODUCED BY CARL REED.

CAST:

Stanley Smith	Stan Stanley
Rodney Terrill	Alan Brooks
Tom Randa'l	Jay Holly
Steve McAllister	William Augustin
Dolores	Camelia Campbell
Ted Arnold	Edgar Barrier
Mary Ann	Elaine Ivans
The Bird of Paradise	Leo Howe
Lester Queen	Lester Sheehan
Edgar "It" Morton	Wally James
Nell Morton	Martha Vaughan
Toto	Ed Hearn
Fritz Otto	William Selig
Herman Otto	Herman Lenzen
Girls with Dolores and Randall:	
Flo	Julie Childrev
Bobby	Margaret Bragaw
Jewel	Anna Keller
Jane	Jane Rich
Bill	Frank Leslie
Bradley	William Cavanaugh
Peaches	Charles Ordway

The Play : *By Robert Littell*

They Don't Come Any Dirtier

TO THE THREE tiresome and unspeakably slimy acts of "Pleasure Man" the police, by arresting the entire cast, contributed a fourth, and even the most rabid opponent of official interference would find it hard to protest on this occasion.

The bulk of Mae West's latest is feeble back-stage melodrama, relieved by some mildly amusing characters and local color. If this were all, "Pleasure Man" would die unnoticed in a few weeks. But it is smeared from beginning to end with such filth as cannot possibly be described in print, such filth as turns one's stomach even to remember.

If all the fifty-five members of the cast had spent every one of their many hours in the Forty-seventh Street police station thinking up ways whereby I might tell you politely just what they did to get locked up, they would be largely unsuccessful. And if you could be told, you would probably become extremely sick.

Nearly half the performers are cast in the roles of what, for lack of a more printable term, may be called "female impersonators." One scene shows them in women's clothes, dressing and undressing. The final act shows us a "drag," or party, given by one of this kind for the others of his kind, and when I add that the dialogue, throughout is full of the revolting innuendo of perversion I have probably said enough.

Trickling along underneath this main theme there is a sort of plot—a feeble, perfunctory thing about a vaudeville Lothario and his loves. But even this commonplace story ends hideously—with the murder and emasculation of the villain.

In the first act of "Pleasure Man," before it gave way entirely to nastiness, there were some moments which led one to expect an echo of the singing waiters and entertainers of "Diamond Lil." Dancers, comedians, chorus girls, acrobats, coming in to the small town vaudeville theatre and rehearsing their acts. Some of these people, particularly the acrobats, were well cast, and were fairly amusing until the good humor wore off and the dirt began to show.

Leaving the dirt aside for the moment (which is about as easy as picnicking in a sewer), the telling of the more tellable part of the story, once the first act was over, disintegrated into the most weary kind of rubbish. There was none of the gas-light glare and purple glamor of "Diamond Lil," none of the coarse heartiness, none of the yellow-covered melodrama.

Pretty nearly the most nauseating feature of the evening was the laughter of the audience, or at least that part

"Pleasure Man"

A comedy drama in three acts by Mae West. Presented last night at the Biltmore Theatre by Carl Reed. Settings by Livingston Platt.

CAST OF CHARACTERS

Stanley Smith	Stan Stanley
Rodney Terrill	Alan Brooks
Tom Randall	Jay Holly
Steve McAlister	William Augustin
Dolores	Camella Campbell
Ted Arnold	Edgar Barrier
Mary Ann	Elaine Ivans
The Bird of Paradise	Leo Howe
Lester Queen	Lester Sheehan
Edgar "It" Morton	Wally James
Nell Morton	Martha Vaughn
Toto	Ed Hearn
Fritz Otto	William Selig
Herman Otto	Herman Lenzen
Flo	Julie Childrey
Bobby	Margaret Bragaw
Jewel	Anna Keller
Jane	Jane Rich
Bill	Frank Leslie
Bradley	William Cavanaugh
Peaches	Charles Ordway
Chuck	Chuck Connors II
Joe	Fred Dickens
Mother Goddam	Harry Armand
The Cobra	Sylvan Repetti
Bunny	Gene Drew
Rene	Albert Dorando
Ray	Lew Lorraine
Billie	Jo Huddleston
Sonny	Walter MacDonald
The Male Jeritza	Gene Pearson
The Varsity Kid	Howard Chandler
Ripley Hetherington	James F. Ayers
Mrs. Hetherington	August E. Boylston
Lizzie	Marguerite Leo
Maggie	Kate Julianne
Tillie	May Davis
Bridget	Mae Russell
Burbank	Edward Roseman
An Officer	Joe Delaney
Pork Chops	Herman Linsterino
Sugarfoot	Robert Cooksey
The Leader	Harry Ford

of it which howled and snickered and let out degenerate shrieks from the balcony. If a first-night audience doesn't whistle or throw vegetables or leave the theatre or call for the steward when such muck is put under its nose, but laughs and laps it up, there is no sense in taking the performers to the police station. The real culprits are on the other side of the footlights.

.Last Night's First Night

'Pleasure Man'—Something of a Description of the Somewhat Indescribable.

By GILBERT W. GABRIEL.

Police around the Biltmore Theater last night did nothing to break up the first Broadway performance of Mae West's new smutch, "Pleasure Man." But afterwards, fortified by fresh air, a good third of the audience regathered in the stage door alley, passed cigarettes and the latest rumors, and waited to see the actual collision of the actors and the law. This extra act was by far the best of the evening.

This present report is probably going to be no more than a supplement to the news of what takes place in the Forty-seventh street police station. So permit it to indulge in some of those evasions of vocabulary which make life bearable to drama critics at many modern plays. What happens to "Pleasure Man" is going to be more important than what happens in it.

No play in our times has had less excuse for such a sickening excess of filth. No play, I warrant, has set out more deliberately to sell muck by the jeerful. And no play, besides that—and this is for me the unforgivable of all its sins—has ever so sagged and dripped under its flagrant load that a fairly funny fifth-rate vaudeville show which starts it off ends up a brutal, utterly unsalted bore.

On a night when two worthy repertory companies were beginning their seasons downtown with reminiscences of Dickens and Molière, here was a new play by Mae West. I had never seen a play by Mae West. I hadn't seen "Sex" or "Diamond Lil." I had not traveled out to the quaint places where they acted "The Drag," the play once forbidden to enter New York alive. But so many chirrupy columnists and highbrow weeklies and fellow playwrights and generally young men had gone Mae West, I fell for the tosh and went, too . . . went as far as the Biltmore, anyhow, and got what I doubtless deserved.

Firstly, I saw a ham-greased imitation of "Burlesque" and about every other behind-the-scenes bunkum since "Zaza" was a centenarian. Secondly, I saw some heavily sprayed melodrama concerning a small-time headliner who, for his sins among the ladies is murdered in a manner too surgical for celebration in anything except the musical comedy just across the street from the Biltmore. Thirdly, much dragged in, I saw a "drag"

'PLEASURE MAN.'

A comedy in three acts, by Mae West. Setting by Livingston Platt. Presented at the Biltmore Theater by Carl Reed.

Stanley Smith	Stan Stanley
Rodney Terrill	Alan Brooks
Tom Randall	Jay Holly
Steve McAlister	William Augustin
Dolores	Camella Campbell
Ted Arnold	Edgar Barrier
Mary Ann	Elaine Evans
The Bird of Paradise	Leo Howe
Lester Queen	Lester Sheehan
Edgar "It" Morton	Wally James
Nell Morton	Martha Vaughn
Toto	Ed Hearn
Fritz Otto	William Selig
Herman Otto	Herman Lenzer
Flo	Julie Childrey
Bobby	Margaret Bragaw
Jewel	Anna Keller
Jane	Jane Rich
Bill	Frank Leslie
Bradley	William Cavanaugh
Peaches	Charles Ordway
Chuck	Chuck Connors II.
Joe	Fred Dickens
Mother Goddam	Harry Armand
The Cobra	Sylvan Repetti
Bunny	Gene Drew
Rene	Albert Dorando
Ray	Lew Lorraine
Billie	Jo Huddleston
Sonny	Walter MacDonald
Ripley Hetherington	James F. Ayers
Mrs. Hetherington	Augusta E. Boylston
Lizzie	Marguerite Leo
Maggie	Kate Julianne
Tillie	May Davis
Bridget	Mae Russell
Burbank, Chief of Police,	Edward Roseman
Pork Chops	Herman Linsterino
Sugarfoot	Robert Cooksey
The Leader	Paul South

and its inhabitants. I've already admitted, it was what I deserved.

But seeing was only half the sickening. The shall we call them female impersonators?—were many, and were made to go through all sorts of perverted antics in various stages of robe and disrobe. What they had to speak was worse.

Perhaps they enjoyed it. The fouler phases of exhibitionism may be interesting to pathologists—but they make for pathetic playgoing, to say the least. And the least said here the decenter. If still curious send self-addressed, stamped envelope.

By now I hear of the author under bail and fifty-five performers arrested. You can't kick fifty-six nondescripts when they're down. But the next time there's a Mae West play I shall rush to all the repertory theaters in town.

Two New York reviews of *Pleasure Man*

UP IN MAE WEST'S ROOM

She Bares Views on Life, Etc., As She Eats in Elevated Bed

(This is the concluding chapter in this thrilling series on the life of Mae West as told by Mae herself to Mr. Sommers. From the days when she was a Brooklyn tomboy, Miss West has been climbing — until today she has reached a climax in her career, making virtuous American audiences cheer sin triumphant.)

CHAPTER VII.

By MARTIN SOMMERS.

(Copyright: 1933: by News Syndicate Co., Inc.)

STEP into Mae West's boudoir, please. Let's visit.

You can't miss the bed. It's so big three people could sleep in it at once, and the one on the extreme left would never find out about the one on the extreme right unless they corresponded. It's mounted on a dais. You have to step from the straight and narrow hallway across an ankle-deep rug and up two steps in order to reach the place where Mae lies flat on her back (authority of Mr. Sidney Skolsky, the mole hunter) when she turns out the light and goes to sleep.

Mae is a specialist in beds. This one, in the spacious, old-fashioned apartment at 72d St. and West End Ave., where she now lives with her sister, Beverly, is one of her masterpieces. Its massive dignity is screened by a Venetian canopy of soft green, shot with gold. The canopy rises into a large, six-point coronet over the head of the bed. Around the base the interlocking wings of prostrate swans are carved in wood. Directly opposite the foot is a huge mirror surmounted by a Mae West crest, designed by the unrepentant, unrelenting sinner supreme of the screen herself.

She Sleeps Amid West Symbols.

The borders of the crest, a ribbon-in-the-wind effect, are inscribed:

"SEX." "DIAMOND LIL."

"MAE WEST"

So Mae West, artiste who has given the public a new movie type—a vicious, murderous, dominant bawd, who destroys men without surcease until the end and manages to profit by it—sleeps with the symbol of the character she has created. It is no more than fair, when you consider with what a roar of acclaim the movie

Hollywood sunshine will do to a gal who once was a charter member of the Broadway Sun Dodgers, Inc.

* * *

WHILE we're here let's ask Mae a few personal questions. They're in order if she's to become part of film history, as the girl who gave the movie public an entirely new type, when the public was crying for one, but didn't know what it wanted.

What about boy friends? It's funny, you know, that Mae, of "Sex," of "Diamond Lil" of "She Done Him Wrong," and of "Night After Night," never once has been reported engaged here or in Hollywood. None of those lynx-eyed Hollywood columnists ever has gone so far as to say that Antonio Whatsis or Brian Tweetleberry now is dancing attendance on Mae West. So what about boy friends, Mae?

"Love 'em all and always have, you know that," she murmurs, sinking those large white teeth of hers in a small steak. "My favorite now? Say, when did you ever hear of me tellin' on myself, huh? I've been smart that way."

What about food?

"I like my meat raw," says Mae, and chuckles. "I mean rare, I mean—

When you enter Mae West's room the massive canopied bed hits you right square in the eye. It's er — (NEWS photo) was renamed as a gesture to Will Hays, grand high chaperon of the movies.

Visiting, we may find billowy Miss West devouring a man's size breakfast in bed at 9 A. M. Or we may find her springing from tumbled sheets and velvet coverings, in one of her flimsy black lace nightgowns, as early as 7 A. M.—it's terrible what that

know what I mean? Funny, but I love it. Once in a while a bottle of beer, but never hard liquor. Never did drink.

"Sure I'm crazy about sweets. Like a lotta home-made pastries and other stuff, though I know I shouldn't eat it."

Clothes?

"Well, you know my stuff on the stage and screen, low necks and smart and tight and all that," Mae relates.

"In the street I always wear smart conservatives. Stick to brown and blacks in the Winter. Pastel shades in the Summer."

Mae has one neat dressing trick that's unique, incidentally. She first puts on her shoes and stockings. She combs her hair and puts on her hat. Only then does she put on her dress. All her dresses are made with special slits to enable her to do this trick. Almost all are very low cut in the neck. The experts say her shoulders are the most beautiful in these parts.

What about music, Miss West?

"Really I don't have much time for music on the side, with all my stage and movie work, and all the singin' o' my own songs, know what I mean? Not much time left —y'know right today I'm doin' five shows a day."

Books?

"B'ographies—that's what I like best. I like. Everything that is true, I mean. Everything that's happened, otherwise I'm not interested. If I wanna read fiction, somepin' that isn't true, I can dream it myself if I want."

* * *

BECAUSE she was a child actress or baby vamp in one show or another from the age of 6— when she impersonated Eva Tanguay—the book learnin' Mae received was pretty much catch-as-catch-can. As a result there are great gaps in her knowledge, as is the case with most self-educated people. Although she has Al Smith's gift for analyzing the character of a casual acquaintance, or sizing up an audience in a split second and giving it the proper stuff for a smash hit, Mae's had

no time for researches into the classics.

They tell the story of the time one of her shows lagged along, as shows will at certain seasons. The press agent had the idea that he could stimulate public interest and attract clamor if Miss West played Lady Macbeth, in "Macbeth," at special Tuesday and Thursday matinees. The budding Phineas Taylor Barnum mentioned the project to the star.

"Okay," *Mae is quoted as answering. "Do you think you can get me a script?"*

What kind of jewels does Miss West like best?

"Diamond Lil"
Loves Diamonds.

"Diamonds," says Mae huskily, and with passion. "Crazy about 'em. Mad about 'em. Always was since a kid. Do anything for 'em —well, I mean almost anything."

Her ambition?

"My ambition is to be juz what

I am—a dramatic star," says Mae. "I've got my public now, you know. Nothing better than one show after another. Yeah, I think I'll stay on in the movies. After all it's the thing now, you know."

And what does she think of California?

"Gees, that's livin' (huskily). Lots of sunshine. Gets you up at 7 in the morning. I love it. Want to live there always, sometime. It's livin', I tell yuh."

Two inside stories about Mae West remained untold when we finished yesterday's chapter in the life of this ever-grinning ever-sinning siren.

Why did she battle so hard in the courts, retaining such expensive legal talent as Nathan Burkan, when she and fifty-six other defendants went to trial on charges of giving an indecent performance in "Pleasure Man"?

It was reported at the time that if all had entered pleas of guilty

(Continued on following page)

SOME OF MAE'S BEST LINES.

The lines Mae West speaks are plenty funny, but nobody who sees her is likely to deny that the lines of hers are her chief attraction. If you don't believe it ask the Paramount people—Kate Smith showed there the week before Mae and she spoke good lines, but the take wasn't so hot by more than half. But what we started to say was here's the tape measure dope on Mae, as compared to classic and modern ideals:

	Ancient Greece's Venus de Milo	Hollywood's Perfect Girl	Mae West
Height	5 ft. 4 in.	5 ft. 3¾ in.	5 ft. 5 in.
Weight	135 lbs.	112 lbs.	120 lbs.
Bust	34½ in.	32½ in.	36 in.
Hips	37½ in.	35½ in.	36 in.
Calf	13½ in.	12½ in.	13 in.
Ankle	8 in.	7½ in.	7½ in.
Waist	....	....	26 in.
Thigh	....	....	22 in.

Mae West in court with Alan Brooks, who played title role in "Pleasure Man," for showing of which Miss West and fifty-six others were haled into court and tried for indecency. She spent her own money freely to fight the case of the defendants, and today she explains why.

Up in Mae West's room

Chuck   Chuck Connors II
Joe   Fred Dickens
Mother Goddam   Harry Armand
The Cobra   Sylvan Repetti
Bunny   Gere Drew
Rene   Albert Dorando
Ray   Lew Lorraine
Billie   Jo Huddleston
Sonny   Walter McDonald
The Male Jeritza   Gene Pearson
The Varsity Kid   Howard Chandler
Ripley Heatherington   James F. Ayres
Mrs. Heatherington   August E. Boylston
Lizzie   Marguerite Leo
Maggie   Kate Julianne
Tillie   May Davis
Bridget   Mae Russell
Burbank Police Chief   Edward F. Roseman
An Officer   Joe Delaney
Pork Chops   Herman Linsterino
Sugarfoot   Robert Cooksey
The Leader   Harry Ford
And the Original Indian Five.
Guests at the Party: Robert De Marche, James Clark,
    Charles Ziatoff, George Cartier, Philip Kirchen,
    Philip Crossman, Richard Read, Fred Carlton, Jack
    Denton, Harry Boner, Rudolph Cormillo, Tommy
    Denton, and Frank Rindhage.

Diamond Lil went on tour, playing eighteen weeks in Chicago. *The New York Times* noted that the love scene between Pablo and Lil had been toned down. Odd as it may strike the reader, the Chicago critics were unpleasantly impressed by the crime content. A salacious imitation titled **Frankie and Johnnie**, built around one of Lil's songs, opened competitively at the Adelphi, did poor business, and was mercifully closed by the police in its third week. According to one paper, "numbers" mobsters and white slavers were shocked at the depravity and sanctioned City Hall in its clean-up; the press congratulated their spirit. **Diamond Lil** consistently got excellent reviews.

In Detroit, *Billboard* reported for New Yorkers on 15 June 1929 that the mayor of the city ordered **Lil** closed on the basis of police response; the uniformed drama critics termed the play "silly and stupid." A temporary injunction was secured and the run was extended till a court hearing could take place.

Variety mentioned on 30 April 1930 that Columbia Pictures had approached Mae as to the cinematic possibilities of **Diamond Lil**. She made a sort of screen test for Columbia, performing two numbers for Columbia's "Screen Snapshots" short series. Columbia finally abandoned the idea, declaring the play was impossible to film.

In August, 1930, Mae went on tour with **Sex**, the *Times* reporting her Chicago engagement at the Garrick on 28 September. Her mother had just died and Mae was grief-stricken.

While on her previous tour of the country with **Diamond Lil**, Mae dictated her novel **Babe Gordon** to a stenographer. Macaulay agreed to publish it. As publicity for the book, the publisher offered a prize to the reader who might suggest a new title for the work in its later editions. **The Constant Sinner** won. The novel went through several printings.

If your response to this book is similar to mine, you won't be intrigued by its characters. You can't really get involved with them.

Their motivations of greed, lust, and survival amid a hostile environment are transparent and, they are, in a sense I suppose, two-dimensional. What recommends it is the style, clear, hard, a powerful naturalism. And the content: there are scenes in it only hinted at by Hemingway and, in the pulps, by Dashiell Hammett. Mae West gives her readers a glimpse into the dark regions of modern society.

I find it curious that her depiction of Babe Gordon and the other women in the book has a common ground with Maugham's stories from that period, save she writes from a distinctly feminine point of view, as Maugham did from the masculine. One thing more: there's no untoward romance, no illusions that aren't shattered, no miasma, no wishing that life was otherwise without acknowledgment that it isn't. Mae's dialogues crackle with the language of the streets as it was spoken in 1930. I regret that she has not seen fit to reissue it for current readers.

When the *Sex* tour concluded, J.J. Shubert asked Mae to adapt *The Constant Sinner* for the stage. There were three acts of six scenes each. Much of the dialogue was retained. A jackknife setup permitted the scenes to be played smoothly without pauses.

The play opened out of town in Atlantic City at the Apollo Theatre on 24 August 1931. *The New York Times* reported on 30 August, "It is underworld material from start to finish, and Miss West handles her role with surety and a sufficiency of wisecracks that provide laughter with frequency." *Variety* on 1 September said among other, less euphemistic things: "*Diamond Lil* was a Mother Goose story compared to this one."

The plot detailed Babe Gordon's marriage to Bearcat Delaney whose career as a prizefighter is ruined through dissipation. Babe leaves him for Money Johnson, who is head of a dope ring. When Money is sent to prison for three months, Babe becomes a pusher in a department store. She takes up with the owner's son, Wayne Baldwin. Babe is subsequently installed in a Park Avenue apartment. Baldwin murders Money upon his release from prison and Delaney is charged. Mae's portrait of modern police techniques reveals that they've traded the magnifying glass for a rubber hose. Guilt is unimportant in the judicial machinery, when a frame is easier. Indignation over these aspects of law and order in America must be a recent phenomenon, as no one objected to them at the time, only praising Mae's realism in knowing the score. Delaney is acquitted through Baldwin's help. Babe settles down with him again, but not without keeping Baldwin on a string just in case.

The Constant Sinner had its New York premiere at the Royale Theatre on 14 September 1931. It ran for sixty-four performances, closing 7 November 1931 after eight weeks. The *Times* found the play dull. On 15 September, the reviewer added: "In a curtain speech Miss West confided to her public that she was not really a Babe Gordon off-stage at all, but was more of the home girl type. She did not, however, confirm reports that she would act next year for the Children's Theatre in *Snow White and the Seven Dwarfs*." Jack Mehler in *Billboard* on 26 September felt the play was for morons. Russell Hardie was singled out for his role. Mehler also thought "it has the makings of a good money show, both for Miss West and the Shuberts, who are reported in on it." *Variety* gave it a tongue-in-cheek review on 22 September, remarking that "the story is more bedside than bedtime,

With Walter Petrie as they appeared at the Royale Theatre in *The Constant Sinner*

En route to Hollywood

in fact it is under the sheets."

Whatever the critics thought of the plot to *The Constant Sinner*, the fact of the matter remains that Mae toned it down considerably for the stage. In the novel, Babe leaves Delaney after his acquittal, going off to Paris with Wayne Baldwin. Bearcat gets a cable from Baldwin that Babe is suing him for a divorce. Bearcat's defense was on the basis of a white man's right to defend his wife from the lechery of a Negro. The cynical ending of the story will make a reader laugh to himself; but, no doubt, Mae was right, and what is funniest to a person alone may be unacceptable in a stage drama.

THE CONSTANT SINNER

A COMEDY IN THREE ACTS BY MAE WEST. BASED ON THE MAE WEST NOVEL OF THE SAME NAME. STAGED BY LAWRENCE MARSDEN. SETTINGS BY ROLLO WAYNE. GOWNS BY JENKINS. PRODUCED BY CONSTANT PRODUCTIONS, INC.

CAST

Cokey Jenny   Adele Gilbert
Harry   Donald Kirke
Lou   Jack McKee
Joe Malone   Walter Glass
Bearcat Delaney   Russell Hardie
Buck   Ralph Sanford
Babe Gordon   Mae West
Charlie Yates   Arthur R. Vinton
Bellhop   James Dunmore
Man-in-the-Booth   Bernard Thirnton
Mr. Gay   Rudolph Toombs
Liverlips   Robert Rains
Money Johnson   George Givet
Headwaiter   Lorenzo Tucker
Waiter   Hubert Brown
Wayne Baldwin   Walter Petrie
Leonard Colton   Paul Huber
Defense Attorney   Paul Huber
Barry Washburn   William Daly
Entertainer ("African Strut")   Paul Meers
Detective-Sergeant   Joseph Holicky
Annette   Leona Love
Clara   Ollie Burgoyne
Liza   Trixie Smith
White characters: Adele Gilbert, Grey Patrick, Christine Wagner, Cora Olsen, George Bush, Harry Howard, George Bloom, Billy Kohut, Billy Rapp.
Colored characters: Marie Remsen, Florence Lee, Allen Cohen, George Williams, Henry Matthews, Harry Owens.

Some six months after **The Constant Sinner** closed, Mae's business representative, William Morris, Jr., with which agency she is still listed, approached her with an offer from Paramount. She was to debut in a film based on a *Cosmopolitan* story by Louis Bromfield. On 16 June 1932, Mae left New York for Hollywood and a whole new career.

Hollywood·Personalia and a Gallery

*"It's hard to be funny
when you have to be clean."*
— Mae West

When Mae West arrived in Hollywood in 1932, a spacious apartment had been reserved for her at The Ravenswood, less than a mile from Paramount's West Coast studio. She's retained it ever since. She commenced a life-style and developed a pattern of activity which has not altered greatly in the ensuing years.

The chronology of her films which follows tells its own story. It is a winding down from the tremendous popularity and originality of her first pictures, through the depressing battle against censorship, to the attempts to adjust her format to new trends, and her ultimate withdrawal from the screen. Mae has always tended to be forward-looking in her personal life. She recognized early that middle and old age are characterized by an increasing intolerance toward change. She has made every effort to avoid inflexibility in her outlook.

In the March 1934 number of *Screen Book* magazine, a noted psychologist of the period, Dr. Louis E. Bisch, M.D., Ph.D., was asked to analyze the girl "nobody no's." He wrote: "Seeing a Mae West play is . . . a substitute socialized outlet for two of the most powerful instincts possessed by human beings, namely sex and ego. Miss West's portrayals are unvarnished exhibitions of both. It gives the audiences, both male and female, a vicarious thrill to behold such instinctive reactions and it decidedly benefits it emotionally. Will the vogue of Mae West last? That, to be sure, is problematical. Screen stars do not, as a rule, retain their audience hold longer than five years no matter how excellent they may be. The picture life of a movie celebrity often flames suddenly but dies down just as quickly. People like change and, if the actress does the same sort of thing picture after picture, if often stales and *she, too.* . . . But Mae West is a unique figure in filmdom and it is more than probable that her resourcefulness will prevent her from giving too much of what might be termed 'a good thing.' "

There is one audience tendency the psychologist didn't understand, if he even knew it existed. Once an audience has accepted a cinema personality as a *genre* in and for itself, all alteration is resisted, violently. This circumstance led to Clark Gable and Humphrey Bogart playing the same kinds of roles during their last years as at the beginnings of their careers. It finished Mary Pickford, when she could no longer play sweet young girls, and Chaplin when he abandoned the tramp. It kept Laurel and Hardy inseparable. Censorship prohibited Mae West from being herself on the screen after the Production Code, and, so, she became an institution through *not* making more movies.

Moreover, Mae's screen work brought about an unparalleled transformation in the motion picture industry in terms of styles, sexuality, and views of women in general. It engendered almost as virile a reaction to the impact of her films as she modified much Depression thinking. She became hated for the very things that others loved about her.

The preponderant image of modern womanhood advanced by the romantic tradition of the past and the popular literature of the twenties, thirties, and forties runs counter to the Mae West phenomenon. Clara Bow and Jean Harlow fitted the "sexy but dumb" orientation desired by those males who rejected the attractions of the "sexy but smart" girls. Even by the time Marilyn Monroe came into vogue, or Brigitte Bardot, in nowise had the popular conception of a sex goddess as a mindless body altered. **The Misfits** (United Artists,

Noël Coward, Mae West, and Cary Grant at her apartment, 1933

As Jenny Wren in Walt Disney's *Who Killed Cock Robin?*

1961) became the public confession of the neurotic despondency and hopelessness of body worship, only Arthur Miller, who wrote it, scarcely acknowledged it for what it was.

A tradition akin to Mae's opposed this trend. It started in the pulps with Dashiell Hammett and was embodied in Hollywood product by Raymond Chandler: the glamorous gold-digger who's crazy. To mention Gable and Bogart again, as two instances, they came to symbolize differing aspects of male disillusionment in women. And it isn't so great a jump from the "sexy but dumb" siren who is a screwy gold-digger to the revolution of the fem lib movement with contemporary women wholly dissatisfied with both the beautiful but useless role they formerly occupied and the put-down of the hard-boiled school.

In June 1933, *Screen Book* magazine ran an article by Bob Moak, tagging him as a detective who had found out about Mae's supposed "secret" marriage to Jim Timony, her lawyer and business manager. Moak gossiped that Timony had a wooden leg. "So skillfully does he manipulate an artificial limb as he moves about with the aid of a heavy cane, few of his newer acquaintances are aware of a tragic accident of a decade or so ago, when he sustained injuries that necessitated an amputation." Mae raised the roof and in the July issue the periodical printed a retraction. *Movie Mirror* the same month reported gleefully: "It burned Mae up! 'They can say anything about me,' she stormed, '*except that I'm Mrs. Timony*!' And for Timony himself, he wasn't half as concerned about the story that he and Mae were Mr. and Mrs., as he was about the whispers that he had a wooden leg. For days thereafter, Timony ran around Hollywood showing all acquaintances that both his legs were real, even if not exactly svelte."

The fan magazines invaded Mae's personal life, as far as she would let them. In her autobiography, she affirmed, "I have never been able to sleep with anyone (!). I require a full-sized bed so that I can be in the middle of it and extend my arms spread-eagle on both sides without their being obstructed." According to the fan magazines, in 1934 she slept in a black lace nightgown. She paid as much attention to undressing for bed as most women do dressing to go out to a dance. When dressing, she first put on her stockings and shoes. Then she combed her hair and put on a hat. Although the California climate may not be exactly conducive to hats, they have always constituted one of Mae's passions. She has a fabulous collection of them to this day and frequently will spend an idle hour or two trying them on in her boudoir, many of which she wears no other place. Then, according to routine, she puts on a dress. Her dresses were made to order in the thirties with slits tailored in them to enable her to do this.

Diet, by her own account, is very important to her. She doesn't make a habit of sweets and, when nervous, will often drink only the juice from a broiled steak instead of eating. In 1934 her favorite dish was reputed to be kippered herring. Despite smoking onscreen, in private life she forewent tobacco and alcohol, and today prides herself on lungs kept clean by air conditioning.

Her eyes are violet. Her hair was brownish, rather than blonde, and in her films she consistently wore wigs before they became fashionable. She loves perfumes and used to spend hours soaking in a bathtub filled with suds and scents. She has done very little reading save biographies

Between Jim Timony and Paramount producer William Le Baron

Lunching with Jim Timony and John Harmel

Mae's famous bed

With Adolph Zukor on the set of *I'm No Angel*

of famous women, books on sex, and since the last World War, books on extrasensory perception.

Mae never has been much of a partygoer or socialite. Shortly after her arrival in Hollywood, while sitting in her parked limousine, she was robbed by a stick-up man. He got a bag containing $3,400, a diamond necklace, a diamond bracelet, two rings, a brooch, and a wristwatch. She had previously stored the jewelry items in a safe deposit box in Chicago. They were valued then at $16,000; they were not insured. The thieves were caught, the loot recovered, and Mae was called upon to testify as a state's witness.

In 1935 she was victim to an extortion plot in which she was threatened with acid burns to her face if she did not pay $1,000. She became a prisoner in her own apartment, with a chain two-and-a-quarter inches on her door. Everyone was inspected before being admitted. Libby, Mae's personal maid at the time, watched her closely. She could no longer shop in public. When Timony took her to the fights, they were accompanied by four bodyguards.

When the pay-off moment came, she rode to the scene with a detective disguised as a woman and sat quietly in the car while the wallet was planted at the designated spot. She saw plainclothesmen seize a loitering suspect near the cache. It proved to be the extortionist.

Mae remained close to her family. Her mother's death had distressed her profoundly, and it took her some time to recover. Her father she situated in a suite at The Ravenswood and, when she bought a ranch in the hills, she saw to it that he spent his final years there. Her sister Beverly and husband, and Jack, her brother, also had apartments at The Ravenswood, which building she purchased.

Mae was attached to Jim Timony until his death in 1954. "My only consolation at losing his long friendship," she wrote afterwards, "was the knowledge that he had lived a good life, done the things he loved to do, had had a colorful and exciting career from boyhood on."

She invested her motion picture money in real estate and other holdings. "Of course," she once remarked, "a woman can marry, anytime. But you got to hold on to fame as long as you got it. You can't let anything interfere. You gotta live for your public. You can't do two things at once. I don't regret it." That was in 1934. It didn't change.

With Arline Judge, Carl Brisson, W. C. Fields, Gary Cooper and two Paramount executives

Night After Night

(Paramount, 1932)
Running time: 70 minutes.

Producing company   Paramount Publix
Producer   William LeBaron
Director   Archie Mayo
Original story from "Single Night" by Louis Bromfield
Adaptation and screenplay   Vincent Lawrence
Continuity   Kathryn Scola
Additional dialogue   Mae West
Photography   Ernest Haller

CAST

Joe Anton   George Raft
Jerry Healy   Constance Cummings
Iris Dawn   Wynne Gibson
Maudie Triplett   Mae West
Mabel Jellyman   Alison Skipworth
Leo   Roscoe Karns
Dick Bolton   Louis Calhern
Frankie Guard   Bradley Page
Blainey   Al Hill
Jerky   Harry Wallace
Patsy   Dink Templeton
Malloy   Marty Martyn
Tom   Tom Kennedy
Escort   Gordon (Bill) Elliott

With Constance Cummings, Wynne Gibson and Alison Skipworth

"Goodness had nothing to do with it, dearie."

(*Note:* **Night After Night** *was released theatrically on 29 October 1932. It was George Raft's first starring feature, and typed him as much in Hollywood as it did Mae West. Paramount Publix, when it emerged from its financial troubles, altered its brand name another time to the more familiar Paramount Pictures. Mention will not be made of this specifically again. However, Mae's Paramount contract survived Paramount Publix to Paramount Pictures to Major Pictures, producing and then financing, for Paramount release. Production began on 22 August 1932 and concluded in September of that year.*)

Current owner world rights: Music Corporation of America
Prints of this film may be rented for home or film society exhibition from: UNIVERSAL SIXTEEN, 2001 SOUTH VERMONT AVENUE, LOS ANGELES, CALIFORNIA 90007

Night After Night was a George Raft starring film. It was the deliberate intention of William LeBaron, the producer, and other Paramount executives to build Raft's image after a likeness to Rudolph Valentino, despite his East Side New York accent. Both director Archie Mayo and cinematographer Ernest Haller consciously sought to capture Raft in a Valentino profile. The attempt even extended to his makeup and how he wore his hair.

Mae West had been in Hollywood six weeks, right from her series of theatrical successes, before she was handed the script to the picture. She was cast as Maudie Triplett. Reading the part, Mae thought it small and inconsequential. She was unhappy with the idleness of the past weeks and offered Adolph Zukor, the company head, the return of the $30,000 he had been paying her at the rate of $5,000 a week if he would release York. William LeBaron, whom Mae had first met while working on *A La Broadway* in 1911, persuaded her to stay, asking her to rewrite the role to suit herself. She did, but the altered part shifted the vital center of the plot.

Archie Mayo had been a professional motion picture director for a long time, but he was without theatrical experience. His concept of the screenplay and the dramatic effect of some of Mae's scenes, and her interpretations, clashed. When Maudie first shows up at Joe Anton's classy "speak," the hatcheck girl remarks to her, "Goodness, what beautiful diamonds." Maudie says: "Goodness had nothing to do with it, dearie." After the line, Mayo wanted to fade and cut. Mae wanted him to keep the camera on her while she slowly ascended the stairs to the upper floor. Finally LeBaron was summoned to the set along with Emanuel Cohen, executive vice president of the studio, to settle the dispute. Cohen suggested that they photograph the scene and, if it didn't look right, they could edit it out later. In her autobiography, Mae comments that the executives liked the line and nearly choked on their cigars during the long walk. For some reason, though, she did not attend the preview, feeling perhaps that she wouldn't like herself in the picture as much as everyone else did: she had seen enough from the rushes. In existing prints of the film, the scene is cut directly after the delivery of the line. The modern viewer will never know who was right.

About one thing there can be no doubt. George Raft, Roscoe Karns, and Constance

With Alison Skipworth and George Raft

"What kind of business do you think I'm in?"

Cummings hand in fine performances; but Mae lifts the picture out of the commonplace of just another Prohibition drama. She gives it a high comic line, an effervescence; she provides a humorous commentary on all of the action, accentuates the social foibles being lampooned, and manages to inject a worldliness into the rather sentimental romanticism of the screenplay and the glamorous, almost make-believe love affair between the two principals. George Raft has accused her on several occasions of stealing the picture. If she didn't do that, she made it much more of a picture than it would have been without her.

Joe Anton is a retired pugilist running a swank nightclub in a remodeled house. Roscoe Karns is his valet, assistant, friend, and alter ego. Wynne Gibson as Iris Dawn is only another in a long line of discarded girl friends. "I'm sick of bein' a pal to a lot of drunks," Joe remarks, getting into his morning bath. "I'm only wearin' a tuxedo instead of a pair of tights. I'd give the joint away." Only he's not so sure of it when Bradley Page shows up with a couple of mugs and tells him to get out of the business. He offers Joe $50,000. Joe wants five times as much. Bradley leaves after an ominous warning. "You'll have some visitors one of these nights. An' speakin' of flowers, Joe— just what kind would you prefer?" Joe says: "Anything but pansies."

Joe is taking lessons in how to be a gentleman from a middle-aged teacher named Miss Jellyman, played to the hilt by Alison Skipworth, who, like Mae, had a wealth of theatrical experience. Their scenes together are splendid.

That night Joe spots Miss Healy sitting alone again at a table, just as she did the night before. He sends a drunk on his way and the two fall into conversation. Joe's "joint" used to be Jerry Healy's childhood home. She has been coming there because she has lost all her money. She's a successful Park Avenue ingenue. Dick Bolton, a playboy and polo player, has proposed marriage to her, and she can't make up her mind. Sitting in her taxi, about to depart, she says to Joe: "You lead a happy life, don't you?"

Joe: Do I?
Jerry: Um, hm . . . the pirates of today.
Joe: That's funny. I just finished reading a pirate story. They stole a lot of women in it.
Jerry: Happy, weren't they? (*Pause.*) Well, good night.
Joe: Tomorrow?
Jerry: All right.
Joe: Dinner?

Jerry: All right. You know . . . you have something you must never lose.
Joe: Do I? What?
Jerry: Something different. I don't know exactly what it is . . . or is it my imagination? Oh, well, good night.

This is the way they were playing their scenes. The next day Joe has an intense, but slow-paced, sequence with Miss Jellyman, preparing for his evening dinner engagement. Mae had always paced her comedy slowly. But when she saw what was going on, she decided that she was going to have to speed it up. The moment Maudie Triplett comes on the scene, things have got to move. She knocks on the door, surrounded by three male companions, and the peephole opens.

Doorman: Who's dere?
Maudie: The fairy princess, ya mug!

Upon her arrival upstairs at the dinner party with Joe, Miss Healy, and Miss Jellyman, she causes an embarrassing disruption. Miss Jellyman is asking Joe about the Five Year Plan in Russia, and Joe is about to give an answer intended to impress Miss Healy with what he knows, when Maudie starts talking loud and fast of how it used to be in the old days when she and Joe went on a drunk and it took five cops to throw them in the jug. After a bit of struggle in diplomacy, Joe extricates himself and Miss Healy from the table, while Maudie induces Miss Jellyman to join her in a drinking bout.

Bradley Page shows up. Joe leaves Jerry to wander around by herself. Page agrees to buy the place for $200,000. Joe tells him to come back next night and they'll sign the papers. When he locates Jerry again, she's in his bedroom. Iris Dawn breaks in on them and draws a gun, giving Joe a last chance to say his prayers. He gets the gun away from her, and Roscoe Karns throws her out. Jerry, overwhelmed by Joe's bravery, kisses him, and then leaves.

Later that night, Roscoe enters Joe's bedroom with coffee.

Leo: Have you gone daffy? Get away from that window. Ya wanna get moon burn? If *you* can't sleep, nobody can.
Joe: Well, she kissed me. She must love me.
Leo: How do you know she does?
Joe: 'Cause she kissed me, an' a kiss is a kiss, ain't it?
Leo: I don't know anything about them women.
Joe: What d' ya mean, *them* women?
Leo: Well, maybe they kiss because they like it.
Joe: They kiss because they *love* it.
Leo: All right, maybe they love it. But maybe they

don't love the guy they kiss.
Joe: Well, what do they kiss 'em for?
Leo: Because they love to kiss.

Leo gets to sleep finally on a couch in the barroom. Maudie and Miss Jellyman are using his bed.

When Miss Jellyman discovers she's slept through the day and missed her classes, she gets flustered. Her interchange with Maudie is comedy at its best. Maudie wonders why she's worried.

> *Jellyman:*   Well, this is my livelihood.
> *Maudie:*   Your livelihood? Why, dearie, you're wasting time. Why a girl with your poise and class . . . why you'd make thousands in my business.
> *Jellyman:*   Your business! Why, are you asking me to come into *your* business?
> *Maudie:*   Why, of course. Why not? One of the best payin' rackets in the world.
> *Jellyman:*   Of course, I recognize that your business has been a great factor in the building of civilization and, of course, it has protected our

good women and thereby preserved the sanctity of the home (*Mae is becoming increasingly perplexed by all this*), and there were such women as Cleopatra and, of course, France owes a great deal to Du Barry and, well, me, dear?—don't ya think I'm just a little old?

> *Maudie:*   Say, what kind of a business do you think I'm in?

It turns out that Maudie owns a string of beauty parlors and wants Miss Jellyman to manage her newest operation, the Institute de Beaut.

Joe in the interim looks up Jerry Healy at home to convince himself she really loves him. Only she doesn't; she's going to marry Bolton, because he's rich and has the right background. Joe tells her off, returns to his speak in a huff, and turns down Bradley Page's offer. Page goes back to his gang and they get out their guns and hop in a touring car. Jerry returns to the club, goes to Joe's bedroom, and starts smashing the place up. Joe finds her and they discover to no one's surprise but their own that they're in love. Page arrives and there's plenty of shooting. The boys come for the rods Joe keeps locked in his closet. Running downstairs to join them, Joe is stopped by Jerry long enough for her to kiss him.

"C'mon, Mabel," Maudie quips to Miss Jellyman, "get out those books—looks like he's gonna take more lessons." With that line the film ends.

Mae got sensational reviews as a result of her performance, which is truly one of her finest. *Photoplay* said: "Wait till you see Mae West. An out-and-out riot, Mae is. It's snappy, and you'll love it." While *The New York Times* thought Constance Cummings "scarcely a girl who would become sentimental about a gangster," they credited Mae with being "quite amusing," which, for them, was saying a lot. **Night After Night** has the magic of the Prohibition period, but it's Mae's gags and her humor that carry the film and make it something special. It was for her only the beginning, and, as beginnings go, an uncommonly promising one.

With Alison Skipworth, George Raft and Constance Cummings

She Done Him Wrong

Paramount, 1933
Running time: 66 minutes.

Producing company Paramount Publix
Producer William LeBaron
Director Lowell Sherman
Assistant director James Dugan
Original play and dialogue Mae West
Screenplay Harry Thew & John Bright
Music and lyrics Ralph Rainger
Photography Charles Lang
Art director Bob Usher
Dance director Harold Hect
Costumes Edith Head
Film editor Alexander Hall
Recording engineer Harry M. Lindgren

CAST

Lady Lou Mae West
Captain Cummings ("The Hawk") Cary Grant
Chick Clark Owen Moore
Serge Stanieff Gilbert Roland
Gus Jordan Noah Berry, Sr.
Dan Flynn David Landau
Russian Rita Rafaela Ottiano

Spider Kane Dewey Robinson
Sally Rochelle Hudson
Connors Tammany Young
Ragtime Kelly Fuzzy Knight
Frances Grace LaRue
Doheney Robert E. Homans
Pearl Louise Beavers
Pal Wade Boteler
Mrs. Flaherty Aggie Herring
Bar Fly Arthur Houseman
Big Bill Tom Kennedy
Pete James C. Eagle
Mike Tom McGuire
Framed Convict Frank Moran
Jacobson Lee Kohlmar
Steak McGarry Harry Wallace
Tout Mike Donlin
Janitor Michael Mark
Cleaning Woman Mary Gordon
Bar Fly (No. 2) Al Hill
Man in audience Ernie Adams
Street Cleaner Henie Conklin
Patron (who hits girlfriend) Jack Carr

Between Gilbert Roland and Rafaella Ottiano

(Note: Released in February 1933, at a negative cost of $200,000. **She Done Him Wrong** *had a domestic gross in excess of $2,000,000. Although banned in Austria after a single night, the picture did more than $1,000,000 additionally world-wide. It was produced at Paramount studios in Hollywood, commencing production on 21 November 1932, concluding in December of that year.* **Ruby Red** *was the working title during the early weeks.)*

Current owner world rights: Music Corporation of America
Prints of this film may be rented for home or film society exhibition from: UNIVERSAL SIXTEEN, 425 N. MICHIGAN AVENUE, CHICAGO, ILLINOIS 60611

The Paramount story department read **Diamond Lil** and commented, "We don't think Miss West's play would make a good picture. The period—the Gay Nineties—would be all wrong for the moviegoers who are college students, teenagers, and children." Things weren't so different in 1933 in Hollywood from what they are today—the fact that the stage play had enjoyed immense financial success impressed almost no one.

It was the Hollywood pattern to secure a new property of seemingly unique interest, decide upon a mode of exploitation, pursue that mode until it was exhausted, and then again to secure a new property. Mae West is one of the few who beat them at their own game. Because of Paramount's dubious box-office prospects, studio brass was more inclined to listen to Mae than was normally the case with an untried talent. Mae's most famous creation had been the Diamond Lil character; she had become prominent because of it, just as Chaplin capitalized on the Tramp, or Jack Barrymore cast himself in the perpetual role of the beloved rogue.

Paramount did bring the play to the screen, despite reservations. It was the Hollywood making of Mae West. She became a national sensation. All the fan magazines ran stories about her, her life, her philosophy. To Ruth Biery of *Movie Classic*, which ran a four-part biography of her, Mae remarked for the April, 1934 number, "I know it won't last forever. It's a question, now, of how long I can stay there. *I know!* A couple of pictures, maybe more. No one lasts forever. I'll get out while I still top 'em all. When I think they've had enough. . . ." The statement was more than prophecy; it was her vision of her career and how she intended to manage it.

What moviegoers did not discern in **She Done Him Wrong**, nor the critics, nor the Paramount executives, was Mae's social insight, her profound, starkly honest perception of the human comedy, her instinctive understanding of people. "I don't read," she said in an interview, "never have read and guess I never will. I write in my books what I learned myself, from life." Audiences enjoyed the gag-lines, the quips, the snappy dialogues, the Depression era songs with a Victorian setting. But Mae's first starring picture has survived the test of time on the broader basis of her fundamental grasp of the human predicament. **She Done Him Wrong** sets forth Mae's transmutation of moral values, her reversal of hypocrisy, and her quest for truth. She sums up her opinion of life in her comment to Cary Grant about his charges at the Rescue Mission.

> *Lou:* Ain't none of 'em worth savin'. If you hang around 'em long enough, you'll get that way yourself.

Critics complained at the time that there was no moral retribution in the film. In terms of conventional values, there isn't. What there is of it resembles life where the loser is imprisoned by his lack of character, and the winner, by means of character, shrewdness, and cognizance of artifice, turns disaster to advantage.

Mae said in an interview to Gladys Hall in *Movie Classic* for August, 1933, concerning men: "I can take 'em or leave 'em. I'm just like a man with my romances—here today and gone tomorrow. . . . Men are conveniences to me, nothing more. If they can help me in any way, socially or financially, I can be nice to 'em. . . . I get my diamonds and my men by being mean to them. I act ill-tempered, I won't talk to 'em. I say I guess I don't want to see 'em anymore. I act so mean they have to do something to put me in a good humor —so they give me diamonds."

Al Kaufman and William LeBaron, producers at Paramount, were walking on the lot with Mae between them, when she spotted, in her words, a "sensational-looking young man" walking along the studio street. She insisted on knowing his name. She wanted him for the lead. Cary Grant wrote of the incident for *Screen Book* for December, 1933: "I first met Miss West one night at the fights at the Hollywood American Legion stadium. I understand that she had already seen me and asked for me to play The Hawk in her picture. It seems that during her search for a suitable leading man she had seen me getting out of my studio car and decided I was the type to play opposite her. I suppose it was because she is blond and I am dark and we make a suitable contrast. Another factor in my getting the role in *She Done Him Wrong* was that Lowell Sherman, the director, had liked my work with Miss Dietrich in *Blond Venus*."

Just what Mae found to be "sensational" about Cary Grant is hard to say, but she was in need of a leading man with poise, reserve, a softness, and a frigidity of demeanor. She got them all in Grant, and she was right in the end—he was to become known as a magnificent screen lover. Similarly, in choosing Lowell Sherman to direct the picture, she got a former

"I Wonder Where My Easy Rider's Gone"

With Gilbert Roland

leading man from the legitimate stage with a trained sense of the theatre and a knowledge of filmmaking that went back to D.W. Griffith in his heyday.

It usually took fifteen to twenty weeks to shoot a high-budget feature. The Paramount executives didn't believe Mae when she told them, at a staff meeting, that it would require just three weeks to bring the picture in. It actually took only eighteen days. Mae rehearsed with Noah Beery, Sr., Cary Grant, and several other cast members for a week before shooting began. This permitted her to adjust stage dialogue to the actors' personalities and to the medium of the screen. Once work on the film commenced, retakes were unnecessary.

She Done Him Wrong is set in the Bowery during the late 1890s; the mood and setting are established through a series of short vignettes and a brief written preface after the credits. Gus Jordan's saloon is a center for drinking pint beer in tin pails, and shady activities. Gus himself is the local ward boss enjoying political favors and Lou's attentions. Dan Flynn is envious of Gus's position and is waiting his chance to topple him. The scene cuts away from Gus's talk with Russian Rita and Serge Stanieff about the white slavery business to Lou, being driven through the streets of New York in an elegant carriage and decked out in her finery. Loved by men, snubbed by presumably upright women, Lou hesitates upon climbing out of the carriage to pat a small boy on the head, whose mother remarks, "Ah, Lady Lou, you're a fine gal, a fine woman."

"One of the finest women who ever walked the streets," Lou returns.

Mae's penchant for one-line gags sets the tempo for the picture in its early stages and eases

70

Top: With Rochelle Hudson, Above: Dewey Robinson holding Rochelle Hudson while Tom Kennedy and Miss West look on.

With Louise Beavers

the introduction of a somewhat large cast of characters. Casting was always one of Mae's greatest gifts in her films, and she selected her supporting players for their acting and their ability to assimilate a part. Most of the gag-lines come off so well because of the facial and dramatic support of which these character actors were capable.

For instance, the interchange with Gilbert Roland, who does a superb job as a fashionable gigolo:

Stanieff: I like best that marvelous painting of you over the bar.
Lou: Yeah, I gotta admit that is a flash, but I do wish Gus hadn't hung it up over the free lunch.

Or Lou's series of dialogues with her Negro maid, Pearl:

Pearl: Miss Lou, you're so rich.
Lou: I wasn't always rich.
Pearl: No?
Lou: No. I once was so poor I didn't know where my next husband was coming from.
Pearl: But you ain't been in the circumstances where da wolf was at your door.
Lou: The wolf at my door? Why, I remember when he came into my room and had pups.
Or:

Lou: Pearl! Pearl!
Pearl: I'se comin'. I'se comin'.
Lou: You're comin', your head is bendin' low. Get here before winter.
Pearl: Here I is.
Lou: Here you is, here you is. What're you doin' eightball, workin' for me, or sleepin' for me?

Or when Lou cheers up little Sally, who wandered into Gus Jordan's in order to commit suicide in his washroom, because she had made love to a man who refused to marry her afterwards, Lou gives her a little worldly advice, based on realities and not fantasies of social decorum:

Lou: Men's all alike, married or single. It's their game. I happen to be smart enough to play it their way.
Sally: But who would want me after what's happened?
Lou: When women go wrong, men go right after 'em.
Pearl: You want to put more petticoats on her, Miss Lou?
Lou: More petticoats? We wouldn't need petticoats at all, if they didn't stuff this furniture with horsehair. (*She pulls a strand of hair from the chair she is sitting on.*)
Pearl: I wouldn't want no policeman to catch me with no petticoats on.
Lou: No policeman? How about a nice fireman?

72

Throughout all the comic interchanges and verbal gags a philosophy of life is woven, a world-view which invites us to take life as it is, nor to change it, nor pretend that it doesn't exist, but to accept it and, wherever possible, take advantage of it. Lou acts toward men the way Hollywood treats human properties; as long as they are on top of the heap, she is by their side. When the shadows engulf them, and life devours them, she has already moved on to her next man.

Cary Grant is running a rescue mission in a vacant building next to Gus Jordan's saloon, owned by a pawnbroker named Jacobson. While he holds revival meetings at night, he spends his days attempting to reform Gus's customers. Gus tries to keep him out of his place, but without much luck. In the meantime, Gus recruits Russian Rita and Stanieff to circulate the counterfeit money he has had printed. Gus has expensive tastes, and it takes money to lavish diamonds on Lou.

Rita sees in the forlorn Sally an excellent addition to the Barbary Coast, and she and Gus take the girl off Lou's hands. Lou is indifferent to what happens to her. Critics at the time of the picture's release were uncertain as to Lou's motivation, but here as elsewhere Lou is satisfied to permit others to pursue their own ends, no matter what those ends, as long as they permit her to pursue hers. She may not personally approve of what they do, but her knowledge of life tells her that she cannot change people from what they are fundamentally, and so not to try.

When she meets Cary Grant for the first time, Lou gives him the eye. He's a new kind of man. "Why don't you come up sometime, see me?" she murmurs to him, in a line which has since become famous. "Come up. I'll tell your fortune." And then, as characteristic of Mae as of her creations, she looks back at him as she starts up the stairs, his hot innocence staring after her. "Aw, you can be had," she says. The scene darkens on Lou the vamp, the temptress, but not without an awareness of the mechanics of frailty.

Spider comes to see Lou in her dressing room and convinces her that she ought to go to the state prison and look up Chick Clark, who was once in love with her and in fact still is. Lou regrets her short memory and his long one. Wishing to avoid tin corsets should he escape, she agrees to see him.

When touring the country with *Diamond Lil*, it was Mae's habit, in each city where the show played, to visit the public buildings, the zoo and the institutions, the insane asylums and prisons. She had read something of modern psychology with interest, and enjoyed visiting with inmates because they frequently afforded her with useful personalities for her literary works. Chick Clark is a classic type, a man who has become degenerate through an *idée fixe*, his obsession with a woman he wants to completely possess.

Walking down the cellblock, Lou recognizes everyone from some place or other. "It's a frame, I tell you, a frame," one of the convicts pleads. "Well," comments Lou, "you're the right picture for it." She turns to Spider. "One of the fastest guys in the business, but he's takin' his time now."

Because Chick Clark stole jewels to make Lady Lou happy, and was convicted for it, she is expected to remain loyal to him. Uncertain of her fidelity, he attempts to secure it by means of threats against her life if she betrays him. Chick has a score to settle with Dan Flynn, who is plotting Gus's downfall; Flynn was responsible for Chick's being caught. The guard breaks up their pleasant conversation which has been running somewhat in this fashion:

Clark: What you doin'?
Lou: I've been workin.'
Clark: Workin'! Heh! Workin' who?

With Dewey Robinson and Owen Moore

Chick, agitated by the visit, cannot wait out his time. Moore does an excellent interpretation, his nerves and musculature writhing and twisting with fury, frustration, and jealousy.

When Lou returns to the saloon, she hears from her maid that Jacobson is going to evict Cary Grant from his building because he can't pay the rent. She invites Jacobson to her apartment above

With Gilbert Roland

the saloon and the dialogue between them comprises one of the best scenes in the film. Lee Kohlmar, who was brilliantly cast, brushes off his pants before he sits down, and proceeds to wheedle and connive with Lou when she asks him what the building is worth. "You means what's it worth, should I be selling, or should I be paying taxes," Lou settles at $12,000, and gives him one of her diamond necklaces. Jacobson questions its value.

"Never heard of me cheatin' anyone, did you?" Lou asks him.

"No," Jacobson replies, "no, not about money."

Lou eyes him quizzically. "Hey, listen, that sounds like a slam. Comin' from you, I'll let it pass."

Lou has him make over the papers so that she is left out of the transaction.

A compellingly subtle and exceptionally well-acted scene is that with Cary Grant when he does come up to see her, looking for Sally. Lou has already been tipped off by Dan Flynn that a Federal agent called The Hawk is keeping Gus Jordan's place under surveillance. Lou doesn't appear to suspect Grant, but her behavior is ambiguous enough to create some doubt. "You come to me to find another woman," she remarks, and walks into her bedroom. Cary follows her. The emotions depicted are complex. Cary, at once serious and circumspect, wants to reassure himself

that Lou knows nothing of Gus's illegal activities. Lou, equally, is on the make for Cary, distrustful, self-controlled. The quiet change in each of them, as they come together in conversation, and fly apart, and come together again, is sensitively dramatized.

Lou: Cigarette?
Cummings: No thanks. I don't smoke.
Lou: Yes, I guess smoking is going to make a man look effeminate before long.

With Cary Grant

Facing page: The famous fight with Rafaella Ottiano. Left, Rafaella defeated.

Cary Grant posing as a Salvation Army man

With Noah Beery

Or when Lou reclines luxuriously, chatting about her diamonds, Cary remarks, "I'm sorry you think more about your diamonds than you do about your soul."

"I'm sorry," Lou responds, "that you think more about my soul than you do about my diamonds."

Cummings: Haven't you ever met a man who could make you happy?
Lou: Sure. Lots of times.

When Cary rises to leave, Lou walks with him to the door, closing it before he can walk through it. She ambles up closer to him, and he leans over to kiss her. She stiff-arms him, opens the door, and nods for him to leave, which he does ashamedly and determined that next time it's going to be different. "Well," breathes Lou, leaning against the door, "it won't be long now."

It isn't.

Lou's next visitor is Stanieff who has come to make love. He gives Lou a pin belonging to Rita and is about to kiss her when Rita breaks in on them. Lou dismisses Stanieff, intending to have it out with Rita. Rita pulls a knife and is accidentally but fatally stabbed during the ensuing fracas. The lighting produces a macabre effect, as Lou combs the corpse's hair, while the police search her apartment for Chick Clark, who has escaped from prison.

Clark had broken in on Lou earlier. He disappeared after she promised to meet him. But upon dispatching Spider to get rid of Rita's body and having a talk with Gus about his white slavery business, Lou realizes the wind is up. Spider, when he informs her that Chick is hiding in the alley, is told by Lou to have him slip into her apartment upstairs. While doing her rendition of "Frankie and Johnny," Lou motions for Flynn to go to her room, which he does, only to be shot by Clark. The saloon is thrown into chaos, as the police begin their raid to round up Gus's gang. Gus is apprehended. Chick, who tries to shoot Lou, is disarmed by Cary Grant and taken away by the police. Cary approaches Lou with handcuffs.

Lou: Are those absolutely necessary? You know, I wasn't born with them.
Cummings: No. A lot of men would have been safer if you had.
Lou: I don't know. Hands ain't everything.

Lou doesn't go in the wagon with the rest. Cary has her climb in a cab, whereupon he takes her hand in his and removes all the rings so he can slip a single, small diamond on her finger. The implication is that they will marry. Lou murmurs to Cary, as she murmured to Stanieff, "Dark and handsome."

"You bad girl," Cary comments.

"You'll find out," Lou both warns and promises him, and the picture ends.

She Done Him Wrong remains, in many ways, Mae's best picture. Whereas **I'm No Angel** is perhaps better as cinematic art, **She Done Him Wrong**, very much resembling the stage play, sets forth sum and substance of Mae's critique of morals and mores. Lou's closeness to Chick, or Gus, or Cary Grant is doubtful. Mae's screenplay permits us to see Lou in isolated completeness, so much stronger than anyone around her could hope to be, because they are all dependent on others; she depends only on herself. They are prisoners of their ambitions and frenzies; Lou loves diamonds, but is self-sufficient enough to live without them if she has to for a time. She is a woman thriving in a world of men, besting them at their own game, because by her rules she at once follows her sympathies and never allows those sympathies to destroy her. She is a conscious, able, sexually alive woman.

Many delightful musical numbers are incorporated into **She Done Him Wrong**, "Silver Threads Among the Gold," done with an Irish tenor and "Pretty Baby" by the chorus, genuinely of the period. Mae sings "I Wonder Where My Easy Rider's Gone" and "A Guy What Takes His Time," which are distinctly from the thirties, and "Frankie and Johnny" in an updated version. The choreography is as engaging as the gowns are dazzling.

What makes **She Done Him Wrong** such a fine film is what it has to say about the strategy of living. The charm of the picture's setting only serves to remove us sufficiently from the characters as to create the illusion that the insight given us into human beings has to do with a different era. **She Done Him Wrong** is a perspective on life. The commercially successful work of art speaks to all levels.

There is infinite subtlety and care in the film's composition, as in the drum roll in "Frankie and Johnny" becoming the shots from Chick's revolver, the rising and falling head of Stanieff's cane as he watches Lou ascend the stairs, the angle shots of Lang's camera, the delicate portraiture of human faces as the camera repeatedly pans the audience during the musical interludes. Like a diamond, Mae's first starring film is hard, sharp, sparkling, faceted in a myriad of varying cuts, focused from a dozen positions, reflecting one basic principle she learned: human beings cannot be changed in their life patterns. Their patterns limit them, compel and control them, and yet, in their midst, Mae, working behind the scenes, paints them as they stand. The highest form of tragedy is comedy, making us laugh at what is immutable and unchangeable and contradictory, for in the anticipation that all is vanity and folly amusement is inescapable. Above it all is that magnificence of personality whence Mae skillfully constructed the character from which Diamond Lil and Lady Lou evolved. It became her most lasting contribution to world literature.

She Done Him Wrong was the first of several

Singing "Frankie and Johnny"

of Mae's films with which she made personal appearances. She organized a stage show for the New York premiere at the Paramount, opening the week of 10 February 1933. Using George Metaxa as her foil, Mae repeated several of the comic sequences from the picture and sang a few of the songs. The bill also featured Cliff Edwards, who accompanied himself with his invariable ukulele, and the Diamond Boys. Both *Variety* and *The New York Times* reviewed it and, apparently, it was extremely well received. It certainly helped in marketing the picture and perhaps added somewhat to its extended engagement.

Among those pictured on Tira's trunk are Nat Pendleton, Barton MacLane, Randolph Scott, and Edmund Cobb as a cowboy in white with horse.

I'm No Angel

(Paramount, 1933)
Running time: 88 minutes

Producing company   Paramount Publix
Producer   William LeBaron
Director   Wesley Ruggles
Screenplay and dialogue   Mae West
Story suggestions   Lowell Brentano
Continuity   Harlan Thompson
Lyrics   Gladys du Boise & Ben Ellison
Music   Harvey Brooks
Photography   Leo Tover
Film editor   Otho Lovering
Recording engineer   Phil S. Wisdom
Sound engineer   F.E. Dine

CAST

Tira   Mae West
Jack Clayton   Cary Grant
Benny Pinkowitz   Gregory Ratoff
Big Bill Barton   Edward Arnold
Slick Wiley   Ralf Harolde

Kirk Lawrence   Kent Taylor
Alicia Hatton   Gertrude Michael
Flea Madigan ("The Barker")   Russell Hopton
Thelma   Dorothy Peterson
Ernest Brown ("The Chump")   William B. Davidson
Beulah   Gertrude Howard
Maid   Libby Taylor
Maid   Hattie McDaniel
Harry ("A Trapeze Artist")   Nat Pendleton
Spectator   Tom London
Rajah   Nigel de Brulier
Bob ("The Attorney")   Irving Pichel
Chauffeur   Morrie Cohen
Judge   Walter Walker
Omnes   George Bruggeman
Sailor   Monte Collins
Sailor   Ray Cooke
Reporter   Dennis O'Keefe
Courtroom spectator   Edward Hearn

At the Hollywood premiere of *I'm No Angel,* with Sid Grauman, William Le Baron and Albert Kaufman

With Dorothy Peterson

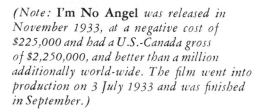

(Note: **I'm No Angel** *was released in November 1933, at a negative cost of $225,000 and had a U.S.-Canada gross of $2,250,000, and better than a million additionally world-wide. The film went into production on 3 July 1933 and was finished in September.)*

I'm No Angel was an unconditional box-office success. Opening at the Paramount on Broadway, it played to some hundred and eighty thousand people in its first seven days, which set a new record for that theatre. A similar pattern in record attendance followed it around the country with extended engagements in cities like Detroit, Dallas, Chicago, and Los Angeles. Depression, unemployment, and social unrest had no effect on Mae West. Indeed, if anything, she was a respite, a distraction.

The film should not be judged only in terms of its time. It is neither contemporary nor dated; it is outside the temporal order. Based on a script by Lowell Brentano, **The Lady and the Lions,** Mae reworked it into screenplay and dialogue suited uniquely to herself. The artistry of the scenario alone would be sufficient to elevate the picture beyond the year of its release and establish its claim for lasting cinematic interest.

Top: With Edward Arnold
Right: With Nigel De Brulier

With William B. Davidson

What helped make Mae's dialogue uncommonly brilliant was how well her resourceful mind profited from her many years of legitimate stage experience. Motion pictures before her time, due in large measure to techniques learned during the silent era, had nearly always depended on visual gags to carry the humor line. Mae was in "talking" pictures and she understood the one-line gag in a way that has never quite been equalled. Audiences, too, from their own acquaintance with vaudeville, the live stage, and, to an extent, early radio, knew how to listen for a double meaning or a catch-phrase. Most of all, Mae knew audiences and *how* to say her lines for optimal value.

At the beginning of the picture, Mae finds herself in conversation with Rajah, the circus mystic, who is gazing intently into his crystal ball. Condensing their interchanges and leaving out dramatic descriptions, the dialogue runs something like this:

Rajah: I see a man in your life.
Tira: What, only one?
Rajah: No, two. I see two men.
Tira: Are they twins?
Rajah: No, two different men.
Tira: Oh.
Rajah: I see a change.
Tira: What? A change of men?
Rajah: A change of position.
Tira: Sitting or reclining?

Most of Mae's finest dialogues are in this fashion—simple, ambiguous, and yet filled with possibilities. One of them definitely didn't get past the studio officials, even before she brought on clamor for the Production Code. The picture was supposed to end with a closeup of Mae and Cary Grant in an embrace.

Clayton: Tell me, do I really affect you as much as you say I do?
Tira: *(speaking through compressed lips)* Put cha self in ma place. Whatta ya think?

I'm No Angel is set in a small-time circus, playing hick towns, with Mae cast as Tira, a sideshow vamp, appearing on the bill somewhat after the human turtle and various other attractions. Living in loose communion with Slick, a professional pickpocket working the crowds, Tira is also expected to perform with the lions after her sideshow stint. Tira maintains a room in a hotel in town where she stays overnight rather than in her dressing tent, and, when the occasion presents itself, as in this case it does with William

Davidson, she has visitors up to her room, in order to shake them down. Slick is jealous of Tira, even though she has lost interest in him. He warns her to stay away from other men, whereas Tira's philosophy is to "take all you can get and give as little as possible."

Alone in her hotel room with Davidson, "The Chump" tells her that she's giving him the time of his life. "Don't say giving," Tira comments, "I don't like that word." Slick breaks in on them and an argument ensues. Davidson suspects he's being taken, attempts to leave, whereupon Slick knocks him out with a whiskey bottle. Thinking he's dead, they abandon him in the hallway, but not before Slick removes from his little finger the diamond ring which had originally attracted Tira to Davidson. When "The Chump" regains consciousness, the police return with him to the circus and Slick is arrested. Tira, worried for herself, gets on the phone to Benny Pinkowitz, her lawyer in New York. Tira needs money and makes a deal with Big Bill to star in the Big Show with a special act requiring her to stick her head into a lion's mouth. It means Madison Square Garden for Tira, and all the swells.

Ingenious casting played a strong role in the success of *I'm No Angel*, as it did with **She Done Him Wrong**. Her control over her vehicles at Paramount was nearly absolute, and, unlike Chaplin in a similarly favored position, at least in the beginning Mae did not depend on a weak supporting cast to magnify her own personality or call attention to her humor. A professional cast, each member accomplished and playing his or her role with passion, lent a credibility to the film, a quality of balance and proportion which only the finest motion pictures attain. The characters themselves are stereotypical, however, in contrast to the excellent actors portraying them; this generates a heightened atmosphere for humor, for everyone's actions are more or less predictable. The predictability highlights the suspense of anticipation; laughter is the relief, as the expected happens within a context of cleverly devised *unexpected* situations. Stock characters are the same as established images in this sense: Chaplin's tramp, built up in countless films, is no less real than what one expects a circus manager to be like, or a colored maid, or a beneficent judge swayed by suggestive feminine pulchritude.

Tira's act with the cats is a smash hit. Mae had always wanted to be a lion tamer since she was a young girl. *I'm No Angel* gave her the chance,

more of a chance even than the Paramount executives wanted her to have. The head trainer had been badly mauled the day before the scene was to be shot, which Mae had drafted herself, where she was to enter the lions' cage alone and put them through their paces. Wesley Ruggles refused to shoot it. William LeBaron agreed with Mae that it would be a good scene, but he refused to commit himself on the risk involved. Finally after much altercation Mae got her way, entering the cage, the lions running through the chute, and men with loaded guns surrounding her in case of mishap. "The lions snarled," Mae recalls in her autobiography. "Their immense paws reached out toward me. I stepped back and cracked my whip again. Then the huge, glorious beasts began their act, leaping from stool to stool, rearing rampant, climbing a ladder and jumping to the ground to follow one another in a line that circled me as I kept cracking my whip. . . . I could see nothing, hear nothing, feel nothing but an overpowering sense of increasing mastery that mounted higher and higher until it gratified every atom of the obsesssion that had driven me."

Kirk Lawrence comes backstage to meet Tira after she has placed her head in a lion's mouth (it was a process shot, with a drugged animal in the bargain!), takes up with her, sending innumerable expensive gifts, one with a card, "To Tira, who can tame more than lions." The romance is ill-fated, though, in that Kirk is engaged to a very proper society girl and his cousin, Jack Clayton, intercedes by going to Tira's apartment and asking her to give Kirk up. The casting of Cary Grant in this role of the man who finally wins Tira's love was again an appropriate bit of dramatic intuition. Cary has none of the characteristics about him that had previously attracted Tira to men.

When she meets Nat Pendleton on her way to the hotel at the very start of the picture, Tira feels his muscles, and comments on them. She makes a similarly overt gesture with Davidson while the two are dancing in her hotel room. But with Clayton all such pretension is dropped. Supposedly not interested just in his money, as she had been with Kirk Lawrence, and apparently in love, she feels his muscles at the end of the picture just before the fade and the deleted line. But in 1933 Cary Grant was thin of physique, not at all the Nat Pendleton type. Tira, a lion tamer, is unaccountably drawn to him, but there is something highly ludicrous about their union, incredible enough for the viewer to have the same impression he has at the conclusion

With Nat Pendleton and Harry Schultz

of *She Done Him Wrong*: Tira cannot stay with him forever. She is insatiable and immortal. From this very subtle, and almost unconscious, cognizance the viewer comes away with that same sense of awe before magnitude, talent, and vibrancy which Chaplin achieved only through dependence on weak casting.

The optimism of *I'm No Angel* is not in its "happy" ending, the life Tira will have with Jack Clayton, but in the viewer's conviction that Tira has been triumphant over her circumstances. Having come from humble origins and little money, Tira has mastered her environment; she is captain of her own soul and has charted her own destiny. For this reason it might be said that Mae represented the truly emancipated woman, the woman who could make it successfully in a man's world playing the game by a man's rules. No less than Vivian Leigh's Scarlett O'Hara in *Gone With the Wind*, Mae emerges as a capable woman. Never once on

screen, here or later, does she suggest that she might be an extremely sensitive person who unavoidably has endured her full measure of suffering.

Tira knows her men well, and so provides animal symbols for them. Behind Kirk Lawrence's picture is a statue of a buck; behind Slick's, a snake; behind Big Bill's, a skunk. When Tira wants to leave to get married, Big Bill tries to dissuade her. While arguing, he espies his picture in front of the skunk. "What am I doing in front of that skunk? They used to call me 'The Bull.'" Mae responds, "To everyone else you may be 'The Bull,' but to me you're just a skunk."

I'm No Angel is filled with elaborate and beautiful costumes and has a flavorful musical content. For songs, "Sister Honky-Tonk," "No One Loves Me Like That Dallas Man," "Goin' to Town," "I Want You, I Need You," and the film concludes with Tira singing the title song, "I'm No

Mae fulfills a longtime ambition to tame lions

With Cary Grant

With Kent Taylor

With Gertrude Howard

Angel." Mae has always kept monkeys around her; she regards them almost like children. Boogie, her pet of the time, managed a cameo appearance and because of his penchant for peeling grapes, inspired one of the most memorable lines from the picture. Tira's interchanges with cast principals are up to the standard set by *She Done Him Wrong*:

> *Tira:* I like sophisticated men to take me out.
> *Kirk:* I'm not really sophisticated.
> *Tira:* You're not really out yet, either.

or:

> *Alicia:* You haven't a streak of decency in you.
> *Tira:* I don't show my good points to strangers.

or:

> *Jack:* Do you mind if I get personal?
> *Tira:* I don't mind if you get familiar.

or:

> *Jack:* If I could only trust you.
> *Tira:* Hundreds have.

No scene in *I'm No Angel* is extraneous. It is interesting, compelling, and enjoyable throughout. Some scenes are played with rare distinction, as that of Clayton's initial visit to Tira's apartment, when she decides to let Kirk Lawrence go, but wants Jack

instead. The camera takes a three-quarter medium shot as the conversation straggles to its conclusion, with both their minds on something other than what's being said. Jack has placed a small photograph of Tira in his coat pocket and, with his hands plunged nervously into his trouser pockets, the suit coat jutting out towards Tira, their bodies swaying closer together as they talk, Tira mumbling, "You'll hear from me." More is implied than need ever be shown.

I should also mention to the reader the strange fact that the most tempestuous love scenes between Cary and Mae were filmed individually and edited together for the work print. Mae would sit on her lounge chair, face the camera, breathe her words of soft romance, emote, melt the lenses, rise, and walk to her dressing room. Some time later Cary would come to the set, sit in a chair next to hers, now vacant, and make love, again with the camera in closeup, but no other object within range. It comes off flawlessly on screen. But it gives Mae's Tira character a "stagey" aspect she very much wanted, because, for all the talk about love in her films and outside of them, Mae is basically cynical about it.

The courtroom scene, as Tira brings her breach of promise suit against Clayton, is classic. Duped by Slick and Big Bill, so that Tira would stay with the Big Show, ignorant of the trick that has been played, Jack contests the suit on the grounds that Tira has had friendly relations with a vast number of men. Slick is there, so is "The Chump," and Kirk Lawrence, and Beulah, Tira's maid.

Tira wins by default when, through a combination of theatricalism and innate understanding of human psychology, she disqualifies all the witnesses' testimony, and Jack, persuaded that she really loves him, drops his defense. As the photographers and newspaper reporters crowd around Tira and Benny Pinkowitz at the end of the trial, a woman reporter asks Tira, "Why did you admit to knowing so many men?" She replies, "It's not the men in my life, but the life in my men."

Following *I'm No Angel*, Mae posed as the Statue of Liberty for *Vanity Fair* magazine, which George Jean Nathan said looked more like "the Statue of Libido." The film further enhanced Mae's

With Libby Taylor, Hattie McDaniel and Gertrude Howard

career and, for a time, she became the most famous, sought-after actress in Hollywood. The fame was justified, for *I'm No Angel* is a very fine motion picture. It has glamor, humor, well-done musical numbers, a strong cast, and a consistently entertaining plot-line. But it has more. *I'm No Angel* has an uncommon, poignant, subtle, and sensitive perception of the human condition, an awareness of the foibles of being human, combining a consciousness of artifice with what ultimately unifies human beings.

There is a moral philosophy in this picture, despite the fact that it was originally criticized for moral lassitude. That philosophy has to do with the admission of a woman's sexual nature, no less legitimate than a man's. It has to do with the comic overtones of lust, greed, and vanity, and their basic futility. But more than any of these, it has to do with what it is, precisely, that attracts both men and women and cements them into a social order, what brings them genuinely closer to each other rather than what divides them. In her very personal relationship with the people around her—to Benny Pinkowitz, to Big Bill, to her colored maids (and their honest regard for her), to her rejected suitors,

Slick and Kirk Lawrence—Tira embraces all of life, and all of man, without hatred or pettiness, but with wit, tolerance, equality, and with personal capability, mastery of herself and her world, the world in which she lives and, by extension, the world in which all of us must live.

I'm No Angel has a basic understanding of man. If it has an enduring quality which distinguishes it above the many components of its technical achievements, then it is this underlying philosophy, this open embracing of the human condition, and Tira's triumph in coping with the countless contradictions life thrusts in her path. Tira believes in astrology, but she practices determining her own fate by making the best of her chances. Maybe she says, "Find 'em, fool 'em, and forget 'em," and "When I'm good, I'm very good; but when I'm bad, I'm better," but beyond the bravado is the fullness with which she accepts life, the readiness of her mind and body to respond to every situation, her total involvement in the world at large, and more, her cognizance of the game of life and the personal generosity of character which we know goes on after the show ends, just as her voice does, singing a song with a persistent beat.

Belle of the Nineties

Paramount, 1934
Running time: 73 minutes

Producing company   Paramount Publix
Producer   William LeBaron
Director   Leo McCarey
Original story and *screenplay*   Mae West
Lyrics   Sam Coslow
Music   Arthur Johnston
Photography   Karl Struss
Film editor   LeRoy Stone
Recording engineer   Harry Mills
Art directors   Hans Dreier & Bernard Herzbrun
Costumes   Travis Banton

CAST

Ruby Carter   Mae West
Tiger Kid   Roger Pryor
Brooks Claybourne   John Mack Brown
Ace Lamont   John Miljan
Molly Brant   Katherine DeMille
Kirby   James Donlan
Dirk   Stuart Holmes
Slade   Harry Woods
Stogie   Edward Gargan
Jasmine   Libby Taylor
St. Louis Fighter   Warren Hymer
Blackie   Benny Baker
Butch   Morrie Cohan
Comedian   Tyler Brooke
Brother Eben   Sam McDaniel
Gilbert   Tom Herbert
Colonel Claybourne   Frederick Burton
Mrs. Claybourne   Augusta Anderson
Editor   Wade Boteler
Leading man   George Walsh
Comedian   Eddie Borden
Comedian   Fuzzy Knight
Beef Trust chorus girl   Kay Deslys
Fire chief   Sam Flint
Extra   Walter Walker
Extra   Mike Mazurki
Extra   Edward Hearn
Best man   Frank Rice
Crooner   Gene Austin
Extra   James Pierce

*(Note: Released on 21 September 1934 at an approximate negative cost of $800,000, **Belle of the Nineties** had a domestic gross topping $2,000,000. James Dugan, uncredited, was the Assistant Director. Before the film could be shown in the state of New York, the final scene had to be reshot. Mae and the Tiger Kid originally were to complete their nuptials without a marriage ceremony; the ceremony had to be included. Paramount Pictures transferred no out-footage from the film when they sold negative and rights to MCA. This is not surprising, as it is not the practice of studios to retain such footage more than three years after production. Shooting commenced on 19 March 1934 and concluded in June.)*

Belle of the Nineties was fraught with difficulties. For one thing, Leo McCarey, the director, was far removed in manner and technique from either Wesley Ruggles or Lowell Sherman. McCarey gained his wealth of comic direction experience working on Laurel and Hardy short subjects and the like. The improvising approach of silent film directors, beginning with D.W. Griffith its finest practitioner and foremost victim, didn't apply to talking pictures. The pacing McCarey used in *Belle* is essentially the same as that of a series of short subjects, as opposed to a cohesive feature. This may explain the divergence in the continuity of plot and flow of action when compared to Mae's previous films.

McCarey shouldn't be blamed for all the lack of continuity. Mae worked on both the story and screenplay. Obviously she had more interest in the atmospheric impressions and musical possibilities of the format than in telling a straightforward tale. Both *She Done Him Wrong* and *I'm No Angel* are engaging as stories; they captivate the viewer and involve him in the characters and their scheming. The plot of *Belle of the Nineties* has only secondary importance. The picture is, above all, a personal vehicle for Mae, a display of her talent and her personality.

Another greater difficulty was introduced by the Hays Office and the attempt on the part of women's and religious groups to censor what their members felt to be immoral and in bad taste. Such groups have little feeling or understanding for the problems of the modern world. They choose instead to resolve these issues by ignoring them. Mae West was at least two generations before her time in her attitudes toward feminine sexuality. While certain church organizations were intent on repressing all mention of the subject, Mae had already passed through the next stage, of pan-sexualism, and beyond it. She parodied prudery and permissiveness alike.

Duke Ellington and his Negro orchestra had risen to fame in 1927, when they replaced King Oliver at the Cotton Club. A series of recordings followed in 1929 and 1930 that established his style of jazz. The ensemble made its motion picture debut in *Check and Double Check* (RKO Radio, 1930), an Amos 'n' Andy film. Since Mae's story started out in St. Louis and wound up in New Orleans, she wanted Ellington signed for the picture. The Paramount executives objected. The Mae West pictures were making money; they would make more if costs were kept down. Just how much money was summarized by William LeBaron, who produced all of her early films. "In the middle of the Depression," he wrote afterwards, "the Mae West pictures *She Done Him Wrong* and *I'm No Angel* broke box-office records all over the country, and broke attendance records all over the world. Her picture *She Done Him Wrong* must be credited with having saved Paramount Studios at a time when the studio was considering selling out to MGM, and when Paramount theatres—1700 of them—thought of closing their doors and converting their theatres into office buildings." Mae's original contract with Paramount for her first three films had been renegotiated before *Belle of the Nineties.* Instead of $5,000 a week, she was now to receive $300,000 a picture and an extra $100,000 for the story. Duke Ellington would cost even more money. Her two preceding starring vehicles had been brought in under $300,000 total negative cost. Now, $400,000 had already been spent before further casting or even a production crew was committed.

Besides, the studio argued, an orchestra was presently under contract. If Mae wanted a Negro band, why not hire a cheap group of Negro extras and dub the music? Mae was obdurate. Finally Emanuel Cohen, whose decision it would have to be, was consulted. Duke was signed.

In the long run, it proved a good thing. Ellington's contribution to the picture is among its most pleasing qualities. Mae's performance with him of "Memphis Blues" still ranks as one of the best songs in any of her films. Another number that has Ellington's touch, and McCarey's, is Mae's rendition of "Troubled Waters." Libby Taylor, whom Mae had brought from New York to play one of her maids in *I'm No Angel*, was signed as Jasmine for *Belle.* She had several scenes with Mae much in the same manner as Louise Beavers had as the Negro maid in *She Done Him Wrong.* Jasmine, chatting with Ruby while dressing her, mentions Brother Eben who is holding a religious revival meeting that night on the river bank. They can hear the singing.

Sam McDaniel as the white-haired preacher of a thousand such sermons calls to his flock:

Who's da cause of all sickness?
The flock chants back: The Devil.
Who's da cause of poor crops?
The flock chants back: The Devil.
Who's da cause of all evil?
The flock chants back: The Devil.
What good did the Devil do for us?
The flock chants back: Nothin'.

I 'se takin' up a collection to fight the Devil an'
Ah wants you all to show me how much you
hates him.

Parallel to this invocation, Ruby in conversation with Jasmine talks of the kindness of Brooks Claybourne, portrayed by John Mack Brown. Brown, an All-American football player whose gentle Southern accent suited the New Orleans setting better than it did the Billy the Kid role he played at MGM in 1930, was getting more money in a featured role in *Belle* than he would receive for the string of low-budget Westerns he made for Monogram during the forties.

Jasmine: Mr. Brooks sure been good to you. Weren't you just a little nervous when he gave you all those jewels?
Ruby: No. I was calm and *collected.*

Mae's characterization of Ruby Carter shows her to be no better nor worse than Brother Eben. Yet she is somewhat more successful in fighting the Devil than he is.

The Negroes begin to sing a spiritual, "Pray, Chil-en, an' You'll Be Saved," that transforms itself into New Orleans jazz when the flock starts to chant, "That's What the Good Book Says." They sway in time to a frenetic beat. Ruby steps out on the veranda and sings "Troubled Waters." The beat of the spiritual is merged with hers in a fused counterpoint. By means of complex process shots, double exposures, and superimposed images. Karl Struss pictorially integrates for McCarey the sequences of Ruby's song with the Negro chant. As it becomes increasingly wild, there are sudden closeups on faces, feverish dancing, the torchlit scene backlighted through reflections from the river. Struss brings off a split screen effect with the revelers, one half their dancing, one half the reflection of their dancing. Ruby's image is superimposed over this. Her song rises and blends with the jazz spiritual, only to drown it out on the sound track, hitting a single pitch as the camera pans a succession of grotesque faces.

The symbolism of McCarey's treatment of the scene, plus Struss's creative photography and lighting, may seem too self-conscious to be ideally effective. Even the meaning is clouded. But there is no denying its technical impact. The screenplay is quite lucid on the point that the contrast is between varying ways of dealing with adversity and evil. The chanting flock loses itself in song. Ruby has a plan in her mind which should restore for her the rightful order of things.

The last song which Mae and Ellington make notable through their collaboration is "My Old Flame." The setting is scarcely as spectacular as that to "Memphis Blues" or "Troubled Waters." The song carries everything by itself. It doesn't need choreographic elaboration. Entertaining a band of admirers in the wee hours of the morning, the men ask Ruby to sing her favorite song. She does.

Since the silent era, Richard Wagner's system of leitmotifs was used in scores accompanying films during theatrical exhibition, the motifs identifying various characters or themes. This theory was further exploited with film stock tinting, with characters assigned certain colors. At the beginning of the sound era, there was some hesitancy about the inclusion of background music, but by 1934 even Laurel and Hardy were using it to fill in static visual comic sequences; the same year it was reintroduced into chase scenes in Westerns. Ellington's rendition of "My Old Flame" is played softly in the background when Ruby, in the picture, actually encounters her old lover, and, again, background filler is used elsewhere to underscore the comic episodes, although distinctly without the Ellington style.

The settings, the glamorous costumes, the expanded cast, all of this added to the cost of the picture. McCarey's direction and the somewhat weak plot structure when combined with this extravagance give the film the effect of a cavalcade more than a composite cinematic experience. I have said Mae was intent on the musical, not the dramatic, aspects of the production. McCarey furthered this tendency with his desire to attain a high degree of spontaneity, for which almost all other values were cast aside. Even if it was a feature film that he was at work on, his agile mind translated it into a series of two- and three-reel segments, with repeated takes followed by a single take. *Belle* can therefore best be appreciated as a picaresque work, its intensely wrought dramatic moments developing from clever subplots surrounded by a far more memorable and impressive song and dance format, unified in the end only because everything was unified in the beginning through Mae's screenplay. The reader perhaps has already detected that certain parts of **Belle** were based on incidents from **The Constant Sinner**. In the vignettes of serious drama, Mae manages to reaffirm and deepen her perspectives on life and society.

Belle of the Nineties passed through a series of title changes, commencing with *That St. Louis Woman* and then *It Ain't No Sin*. Much of the advance publicity for the film was issued under the latter title. No matter what it was called, it was still bound to be a financial winner. Word of mouth reaction to *She Done Him Wrong* had skyrocketed *I'm No Angel* attendance. The public anxiously awaited a sequel, and *Belle* was easily an attempt to combine the atmosphere and ribald humor of the one with the glamour and enthusiasm of the other. The film emerged as a compromise in another sense, though, thanks largely to the Hays Office.

Truly successful comedy comes as a result of carefully building a situation, in this instance to a high hilarity. Roger Pryor, playing the Tiger Kid, a prizefighter in love with Ruby Carter, is in the audience during Ruby's first number. Opening with a heavy-hoofed assemblage of chorus girls singing, "Here We Are—The Beauties of the South," closeups of Pryor tell us he is amused but anxious for Ruby to appear on stage. Ruby is being readied for her entrance. "You know," remarks her fitter, "when I had an act like yours, I had every man in town at my feet." "At your *feet?*" Ruby exclaims. "I'd rather have them around my neck."

Mae's act is fantastic. Wrapped in a tight-fitting gown, she poses, in turn, in front of a giant butterfly, a bat, a rose, a spider, and, finally, with torch in hand, imitates the Statue of Liberty, while Gene Austin on the track croons the words to "My American Beauty." Nearly forty years later, publicity stills of Mae would be issued in conjunction with *Myra Breckinridge* wearing her Statue of Liberty outfit. Over the intervening time, filmmakers had furthered the display of the body, the admission of sexuality on the screen, the commission of all sorts of sexual acts, normal and perverse, but Mae's dialogue was still censored. Can it be that anything may be *shown*, but not as yet dare anything be said? The body may be stimulated, but the mind cannot be incited to question?

After the performance, Ruby and the Tiger Kid head for Ruby's apartment, only to be met on the front steps by James Donlan, as Kirby, the Kid's fight manager. Kirby is irked at the Kid's infatuation with Ruby. He claims the Kid is neglecting his training, what with his late hours and seeing Ruby all the time. (This is the strongest parallel with *The Constant Sinner*.) They leave

With Duke Ellington and his Orchestra

With Roger Pryor

Kirby outside and retire to Ruby's apartment.

It starts to rain. Ruby suggests that Tiger throw Kirby an umbrella. He is pacing back and forth in front of the building. While the Kid searches for an umbrella, Ruby phones the police and tells them that a suspicious character is outside in the street and they had better pick him up before he does something desperate. About all Kirby has a chance to do is open the umbrella when he is promptly marched off to the station house. Tiger tells Ruby that he loves her. He wants no other man to come between them. He will love her all the time. "Do you mean," Ruby asks, "that I'll have to give up my art?" Again the Kid assures her that he will devote himself to loving her. "If you do that," Ruby sighs, "I'll have to give it up."

Before the censors got to it, this scene was to be followed by a series of time lapses. Kirby mentioned a bout coming up Friday, several days hence. The lapses were to record how Tiger spent those days. The implication, naturally, was that he was being a full-time lover to Ruby. The censors felt the lapses too suggestive, and they were cut out of the picture. As the negative now has it, following their passionate scene together, the Kid just leaves Ruby's apartment and walks into the night. Nearly ten minutes were spent preparing the viewer for a laugh that isn't there. Many of the more amusing innuendoes in the film have also been deleted. They are, sadly, lost forever.

With John Miljan

With Johnny Mack Brown, James Pierce and Harry Woods

Through a clever ruse, Kirby manages to estrange the Kid from Ruby, having him think that she is intimate with several other men. Ruby, to drown her sorrow, signs a contract which will take her to New Orleans and Ace Lamont's Sensation House. Ace fixes up a gorgeous suite for Ruby. Molly Brant, Ace's girl friend, played by Katherine DeMille, seethes with jealousy. Ace meets Ruby at the steamboat. On the way to the carriage, he attempts to make conversation.

Ace: You were born in St. Louis. What part?
Ruby: Why . . . all of me.

Ruby drops her handkerchief so that John Mack Brown might retrieve it. Their eyes meet and they will see more of each other.

Once at the Sensation House, Ace shows Ruby around.

Ruby: Mmm, lovely painting. One of your ancestors?

With Johnny Mack Brown

With photographer Karl Strauss

Ace: This one in particular is an old master.
Ruby: Looks more like an old mistress to me.

After her evening performance, Ace becomes profoundly infatuated with Ruby. When he gets her alone, he tells her how wild he is about her. "The wildest men make the best pets," Ruby remarks, having earlier made the comment to Ace that "a man in the house is worth two in the street."

Ace: I must have your golden hair, fascinating eyes, alluring smile, your lovely arms, your form divine....
Ruby: Wait a minute. Wait a minute! Is this a proposal or are you taking an inventory?

Ruby puts Ace off and returns to the gambling salon and the roulette table. John Mack Brown is there with a pile of chips. He approaches Ruby. "Make your play," Ruby tells him. He starts making a pass, thinks better of it, looks instead at his chips, places a bet, and loses. "That's roulette for you," Ruby quips.

Brooks Claybourne showers Ruby with diamonds, so much so that she becomes quite independent of Ace. When Ace discovers that the fighter he has scheduled to meet the champ has ditched him, he goes to the gymnasium. He finds the Tiger Kid and Kirby, who have just arrived. Ace hires the Kid to replace Lefty Dugan, but asks him for his assistance in raising money. Claiming that he is victim to a female blackmailer, Ace has the Kid stage a holdup while he and Ruby are taking a night ride along the river. Ruby is suspicious when she notices that only *her* diamonds are stolen. Ace's diamond ring is left untouched. Her suspicions are confirmed with she sees the Kid passing Ace the diamonds, which he deposits in his safe.

Ruby meets the Kid and they suddenly realize that Kirby framed the whole thing in order to keep them apart. Ruby keeps her distance from the Kid, though, memory of the theft fresh in her mind. His attempt to make passionate love to her, to kiss her while she puffs on a cigarette, is fine comedy.

During preparations to attend the championship fight, Ruby asks Ace to protect what jewels she still has, spying on him through opera glasses and recording the combination to his safe. Ace has bet heavily on the Kid. For the first twenty-six rounds, it looks as though the Kid will win, until Ruby deftly slips a mickey into his water bottle. The Kid is knocked out and Ace is ruined. Kirby observes Brooks collecting money from bets

Katherine De Mille

With John Miljan

he made on the champ, reclaiming most of his losses at Ace's. Ruby is credited with having given him the winning tip. When the Kid hears this, he enters Ruby's suite in a fury only to have her deflect him against Ace, now believing that Lamont drugged his water bottle. He charges in on Lamont and kills him in the struggle. Before Ruby can get away, the Kid corners her and accuses Lamont of having put him up to the theft, not knowing that it was Ruby from whom he was stealing. Ace had planned to burn down the Sensation House and beat it with Ruby. Ace's room has been drenched with kerosene. While getting her jewels from Ace's safe, Ruby inadvertently sets the place on fire. She escapes with the Kid, first letting Molly out of the closet where Ace locked her in. When Ruby tries to call the fire department, the line is busy.

The story ends happily with Ruby and the Kid at the altar, the Kid exonerated of Ace's death.

There are brilliant lines in *Belle*. Mae tells Jasmine that "I'm just gettin' even with two guys that are so low they could walk under that door without taking their hats off." She says to the men in the bar, "It's better to be looked over than overlooked."

"I've never believed in going haywire on stage or screen," Mae has written concerning censorship. "Obviously, no medium of mass entertainment can be allowed to throw all restraint out the window. Strict censorship, however, has a reverse effect. It creates resentment on the part of the public. They feel that their freedom of choice is being dictated. They won't have their morals legislated by other than criminal law. The professional reformers, the organized pressure groups, the easily impressed do-gooders, can look upon the enormous obscenity that is war and do very little that is effective." *Belle of the Nineties* would have been a lot funnier more of the time if the Hays Office hadn't protected moviegoers.

By modern standards most of these deletions from *Belle* are of mild and innocuous material. Yet, viewed optimally as a cavalcade, for the music, choreography, and glamour, not so much for the story, *Belle* is an entertaining and exuberant film. What it lacks is only significant when compared to Mae's earlier pictures. It is excellent musical comedy, filled with honest frivolity, atmosphere, and several unforgettable songs.

Goin' to Town

Paramount, 1935
Running time: 74 minutes

Producing company   Paramount Pictures
Production unit   Major Pictures
Producer   William LeBaron
Director   Alexander Hall
Assistant director   James Dugan
Original story   Marion Morgan & George B. Dowell
Screenplay and dialogue   Mae West
Lyrics   Irving Kahal
Music   Sam Fain
Gags   Gil Pratt
Art director   Hans Dreier & Robert Usher
Costumes   Travis Benton
Photography   Karl Struss
Film editor   LeRoy Stone
Recording engineer   M.M. Paggi

CAST

Cleo Borden   Mae West
Edward Carrington   Paul Cavanagh
Winslow   Gilbert Emery
Mrs. Crane Brittony   Marjorie Gateson
Taho   Tito Coral
Ivan Valadov   Ivan Lebedeff
Buck Gonzales   Fred Kohler, Sr.
Fletcher Colton   Monroe Owsley
Young Fellow   Grant Withers
Signor Vitola   Luis Alberni
Senior Ricardo Lopez   Lucio Villegas
Dolores Lopez   Mona Rico
Foreman of ranch   Wade Boteler
Donovan   Paul Harvey
Laughing Eagle   Joe Frye
Annette   Adrienne D'Ambricourt
Buck's gang   Tom London, Syd Saylor, Irving Bacon, Bert Roach
Sheriff   Francis Ford
Bartender   Dewey Robinson
Bet taker   Julian Rivero
(Extras: Stanley Price, Andre de Seganola, Bert Morehouse, Morgan Wallace, Tom Ricketts, Sheldon Jett, Pearl Eaton, J.P. McGowan, Jack Pennick, Sam Stein, James Pierce, Max Lucke, Leonid Kinsky, O.M. Steiger, Myra Royl, Tom Monk, Paulette Paquette, James Cowles, Harold Entwhistle, Lew Kelly, George Guhl, Virginia Hammond, Neil Craig, Laura Tredwell, Cyril Ring, Frank Mundin, Eugene Berden, Frank Corsara, Germaine DeNeel.)

With Fred Kohler

At the bar with Syd Saylor, Fred Kohler, Jack Pennick, James Pierce, Dewey Robinson, and others.

The continuing success of her films brought Mae wealth, immediate recognizability, and a triumph of personality. It became the proper thing to seek out and talk to Mae West. Viscount and Lady Byng, arriving for tea, invited Mae to attend King George's Silver Jubilee in London, which she declined. Indian sultans called on her, the rich domestic set from Mrs. Reginald Vanderbilt to Lady Furness. She even got a visit from President Roosevelt's playboy son, Elliott, along with health food addicts and weight-lifters.

*(Note: **Goin' to Town** was released theatrically on 17 May 1935. It exceeded, in number, the casts of any of Mae's previous films. Production commenced on 18 December 1934 and concluded in February 1935.)*

Current owner world rights: Music Corporation of America
Prints of this film may be rented for home or film society exhibition from: UNIVERSAL SIXTEEN, 425 N. MICHIGAN AVENUE, CHICAGO, ILLINOIS 60611

On the Paramount lot, Emanuel Cohen organized a separate production unit for the Mae West pictures at the conclusion of *Belle of the Nineties*. Her Paramount contract had several generous provisions added to it. Mae's earnings resulted in a unique situation. Her personal revenue forms for 1933 indicated that she grossed $229,840, $344,160 in 1934, and $480,833 in 1935. Of her 1935 income, which Cohen's reorganization made possible, the Federal Government claimed $234,000, the state of California $50,050, and Mae netted all of $155,050. This was before taxes escalated! She remained the foremost working woman in the United States, a position held for men by William Randolph Hearst.

William LeBaron was retained as executive producer for her films. Marion Morgan and George B. Dowell wrote an original story which Mae adapted to suit herself as a screenplay. In addition to scripting the usual witty dialogue, Mae chose to parody the life-style and mores of the wealthy and titled classes as she was coming to know them.

The overall production budget was somewhat curtailed from what it had been with *Belle of the Nineties*. The first working title for the film was *Now I'm a Lady*, which made its intent more apparent than the new title given it near completion in February of *How Am I Doin'*. By the middle of March, the title was changed finally to *Goin' to Town*.

The strictly suggestive elements in her earlier pictures were reduced to a minimum in *Goin' to Town*. It also differed from the former entries in that it was concerned more with Mae in society than with Mae as an individual, although Mae was still the center of the film. The strong casting was again a significant factor in its cinematic scucess.

The songs weren't really elaborate numbers, with the possible exception of "My Heart at Thy Sweet Voice," which found Mae in the operatic role of Delilah in a scene from Saint-Saens' opera. "He's a Bad, Bad Man, but He's Good For Me" had Fred Kohler, Sr., in mind. At the time, he was probably one of the most familiar Hollywood Western heavies in Paramount melodramas, as well as films for other studios. "Love Is Love in Any Woman's Heart" was directed toward Paul Cavanagh and the passionate song "Now I'm a Lady" described how she lured him.

Mae liked Westerns. *Goin' to Town* was her first. At least, it started out West, even if it didn't end up there. The attraction was mutual, perhaps, because Ken Maynard was so taken with her pictures that he had a typical Mae West setting scripted into his *Honor of the Range* (Universal, 1934), with heavy-hoofed chorus girls doing a Gay Nineties routine and himself singing 'She's Only a Bird in a Gilded Cage." Mae was given lariat lessons and the scenario called for her, early in her pursuit of Cavanagh, to take the direct course by shooting his hat off when he wouldn't pay attention to her, and roping him when he tries to walk away.

Goin' to Town, due to its intricate plot, had a wide assortment of characters. Opening to Fred Kohler, as Buck Gonzales, riding into town with his gang and stopping at the local dance emporium, Buck and his boys crowd around the bar. They are decidedly bad hombres. Buck asks where Cleo is, and the camera cuts to Cleo in Grant Withers' arms, sitting safely behind a curtained table on the second floor. Withers is getting turned on.

> *Withers:* What excuse has a gal like you for running around single?
> *Cleo:* I was born that way.

Withers attempts to persuade Cleo to marry him, when word comes that Buck has just pulled in. Cleo gets up and Withers follows her down the steps to the crowded dance floor where a hot jazz number is being played. They take a turn around the floor as Cleo sings her first song.

Buck pushes his way over to her and grabs her out of Withers's arms. Withers grabs her back. Buck pulls her to him again. Cleo throws them both off. Buck tells Withers to scram and takes Cleo with him in the direction of the back room.

> *Buck:* Any other dame and I wouldn't give a hoot, but with you I'm dynamite.
> *Cleo:* Yeah, an' I'm your match!

Buck is busy celebrating with Cleo and the boys when the sheriff enters to warn him against any further rustling. Buck swears he knows nothing about it. While Cleo walks toward her dressing room, she remarks to a crony that she won Buck in a crap game. She loses him in the next scene where, running stolen cattle, Buck is shot by the sheriff. Buck falls with his head under water in a stream, the camera cutting to a perplexed steer watching the proceedings, then to another steer's head on a barn at Buck's ranch the day of his proposed wedding to Cleo. Cleo arrives in a big car and is saddened to learn of Buck's passing. Paying her last respects, she meets Winslow, Buck's business manager, and shows him the document Buck signed deeding the whole place to her in exchange for marrying him. She has shown good intention, and the court awards the property to her by default. She becomes one of the wealthiest women in the state.

Retaining Winslow to manage her interests and keep an eye on the cattle while she is minding the men, Cleo takes a short horseback ride around her new holdings with Wade Boteler accompanying her. Cactus is a horse fit for racing, if duly frightened by gunfire. Cleo thinks she might race him, but is more interested in the English geological engineer drilling her prospective oil wells. This sequence was shot near a derrick at Newhall that had been used earlier in the serial *The Vanishing Legion* (Mascot, 1931) where Harry Carey was bringing in a gusher. Cleo falls hard for Carrington. At their first meeting, out by the derrick, Carrington is somewhat cool toward Cleo, feeling her to be mere "crude oil." It is here that Cleo shoots his hat off when he ignores her.

> *Carrington:* Look here—what do you mean by shooting at me? I don't happen to be a target, you know. Not even for somebody like you.
> *Cleo:* Hmm, what do you know about me?
> *Carrington:* Just what I see, and that's quite sufficient.
> *Cleo:* You're easily satisfied.
> *Carrington:* What do you want with me—?
> *Cleo:* Nothin' . . . yet!
> *Carrington:* You possess an extraordinary sense of humor.
> *Cleo:* Yes . . . an' that ain't all.
> *Carrington:* I'm afraid you'll have to excuse me. I'm rather busy for this sort of chit-chat.
> *Cleo:* Owww! English, huh?
> *Carrington:* Yes, do you mind?
> *Cleo:* Noooo, I raaather like it.
> (*He turns and walks away.*)
> *Cleo:* Give me room, boys.

Cleo ropes Carrington and draws him to her. He is disgusted at the spectacle, while everyone is laughing. On the way back, Cleo tells Winslow and Wade Boteler to see that Carrington gets over to the ranch house that night and he should bring his blueprints with him.

When he arrives, Cleo has already wagered with Boteler and Winslow that she'll win Carrington over. Once more, as in *I'm No Angel*, when Tira sets out to charm Cary Grant, the scene between her and Carrington is a fine detailing of mutual hostility and interest.

> *Cleo:* I'll admit I was a little crude, but you like me.

Between Karl Strauss and Alexander Hall, the director

> *Carrington:* I admire your conceit.
> *Cleo:* I know you've been used to dames who serve pink tea an' stick out their little fingers when they drink it. Well, I like yuh anyway.
> *Carrington:* You know, this is the first time I ever came in contact with a woman like you.
> *Cleo:* If I can help it, it won't be the last. Now, I can be different. If I want to. You ain't seen my better side.
> *Carrington:* You're a dangerous woman.
> *Cleo:* Thanks.

Boteler and Winslow break in on them and, finding out about the bet, Carrington walks off in a huff. Cleo still figures she can win him over, until Winslow tells her that Carrington's oil-drilling company is sending him to Buenos Aires. She decides she will follow him, racing Cactus in the

The stable scene: from left to right Joe Frye, Tito Coral, Mae West, Paul Cavanagh, and Mona Rico.

sweepstakes. She picks up a copy of *Town and Country* magazine and shows Winslow a picture of Mrs. Crane Brittony. If that's a lady, and that's what it takes to win Carrington, Winslow's got to teach her the ropes.

Cleo becomes the talk of Buenos Aires, particularly since her oil wells have come in, making her fabulously wealthy. Upon seeing Mrs. Crane Brittony, she immediately suggests a side bet on Cactus winning the race. Mrs. Brittony pays Ivan, her gigolo, to drug Cactus the night before the race, but Taho, the trainer, scares him off. Cactus catches cold in the process, so the day of the race Cleo has Taho stand down near the finish line with a revolver to frighten the horse sufficiently to win. She meets Carrington who is with friends in the box next to hers, and Ivan, feeling he has a better chance with Cleo, joins her entourage.

The race footage is quite exciting. There are magnificent running inserts and a very effective closeup of the three horses nearing the finish line, neck-and-neck. Cactus, terrified by the revolver shots, edges ahead at the last minute to win.

At the victory dinner, Cleo makes a few remarks, while Carrington takes a swing at Ivan when he overhears him bragging to friends that he plans to marry the Cleo Borden millions. After the ruckus, Cleo pulls Ivan aside to wise him up. "We're intellectual opposites," she tells him. "I'm intellectual, and you're opposite."

"I'm an aristocrat and the backbone of my family," Ivan insists.

"Then your family'd better see a chiropractor," Cleo responds.

In a last-ditch effort to gain respectability in her suit with Carrington, Cleo has Winslow seek out a man with a name and background for a purely "business" marriage. He comes up with Fletcher Colton, Mrs. Crane Brittony's nephew, who was about to commit suicide over losses at

Between Ivan Lebedeff and Marjorie Gateson.

With Lobedeff, Vladamir Bykoff, Gilbert Emery and Paul Cavanagh

roulette. They are wed and head back to Southampton and the Colton estate. Inside Colton Manor, the camera pans back from a life-size figure of Antinous, Emperor Hadrian's lover, and Cleo welcomes Mrs. Brittony and her friends. The conversation is short and cold. But, Cleo assures Winslow, they'll show up for her gala evening, especially as she is planning on throwing an opera with herself singing the part of Delilah, "a female barber that made good."

In the meantime, Mrs. Crane Brittony hires a detective agency to "prove" that Cleo is a woman of ill-repute. To force the issue, they pay Ivan's way from South America and intend to have him found hiding in Cleo's room. That night Carrington shows up at the ball, now an earl. He declares his love to Cleo and begs her to marry him.

With Gilbert Emery, Tom Monk, Tito Coral and Marjorie Gateson

With Gilbert Emery

With Luis Alberni

Monroe Owsley on the floor, Tito Coral and Ivan Lebedeff

As Delilah

With Paul Cavanagh

Colton, in need of money to pay off a gambling debt, opens Cleo's safe and sees Ivan lurking in the gloom. They struggle and Colton is killed by the gun he was holding. Ivan runs onto the porch and hides again.

The opera is in full swing, used throughout these scenes as surprisingly appropriate background music. Cleo does her number, caressing Samson's locks lovingly and singing the difficult aria in fine style. When she returns to her bedroom during intermission, she finds Colton's body and also discovers Ivan, who left a monogrammed cigarette in an ashtray. The planted detective tries to cast blame on Cleo, but Taho apprehends the fleeing Ivan and forces him to talk. Ivan implicates Mrs. Crane Brittony and tells everything, totally discrediting her. The picture ends happily with Cleo now married to Carrington, the Earl of Stratton.

Goin' to Town is an entertaining, buoyant, lively film with the emphasis on plot and social mores. The songs and musical numbers are never the center of the drama, as they had been in **Belle of the Nineties**. In this film Mae brought her critique of society into a wholly new perspective. Just as Negro maidservants had been her most trusted confidants in earlier films, so the Indians Taho and Laughing Eagle, the latter her jockey, are her most reliable aids here. Mae looks at society straight on, piercing the seemingly impenetrable barriers of class with her wit. Her revaluation of values distills the good from the nobility and redefines it as something not associated with breeding or family, but with character and personal competence. *Goin' to Town* closes out with a song, "Now I'm a Lady," the words "Come up and see me sometime" trailing and lingering after the fade.

With Harold Huber

Klondike Annie

Paramount, 1936
Running time: 77 minutes

Producing company   Paramount Pictures
Production unit   Major Pictures
Producer   William LeBaron
Director   Raoul Walsh
Assistant director   David MacDonald
Original story   Mae West
Story ingredients   Marion Morgan & George B. Dowell
Material suggested by   Frank Mitchell Dazey
Screenplay and dialogue   Mae West
Music and lyrics   Gene Austin & Jimmie Johnson
Interior decorations   A.E. Freudeman
Art directors   Hans Dreier & Bernard Herzgrup
Photography   George Clemens
Film editor   Stuart Heisler
Recording engineer   Harold Lewis & Louis Mesenkop

CAST

The Frisco Doll (Rose Carlton)   Mae West
Bull Brackett   Victor McLaglen
Jack Forrest   Phillip Reed
Annie Alden   Helen Jerome Eddy
Brother Bowser   Harry Beresford
Chan Lo   Harold Huber
Big Tess   Lucille Webster Gleason
Vance Palmer   Conway Tearle
Fanny Radler   Esther Howard
Fah Wong   Soo Yong
Buddie   John Rogers
Grigsby   Ted Oliver
Sir Gilbert   Lawrence Grant
Organist   Gene Austin
Marinoff   Vladimir Bykoff
Lun Fang   Tetsu Komai
Bartender   James Burke
Quartermaster   George Walsh
Ship's cook   Chester Gan
Second mate   Jack Daley
Third mate   Jack Wallace
Extra   Philo McCullough

With heavyweight champion James J. Braddock and Raoul Walsh

(Note: **Klondike Annie** *was released 21 February 1936 at an approximate negative cost of $1,000,000. A prerelease running time of 85 minutes was clocked at the film's preview showing. Deletions from the negative give all existing prints a running time of 77 minutes. Production began on 16 September 1935 and concluded in December of that year.)*

Current owner world rights: Music Corporation of America
Prints of this film may be rented for home or film society exhibition from: UNIVERSAL SIXTEEN, 425 N. MICHIGAN AVENUE, CHICAGO, ILLINOIS 60611

No motion picture Mae West was ever in has caused so much controversy for all the wrong reasons as *Klondike Annie*. It unleashed an outraged cry from numerous pious women's groups, spearheaded by a vicious attack from that self-appointed guardian of American morality in the thirties, William Randolph Hearst. It was totally misunderstood in its time. But even with the subsequent deletions, this film remains her best.

At the sneak preview at the Alexandre Theatre in Hollywood the audience was in a state of shock when the Frisco Doll kills Chan Lo in self-defense, and once more when she paints the face of a dead missionary in the gaudy hues of a prostitute. The Paramount executives, terrified lest this reaction ruin the box-office potential, deleted these portions of the film from the negative. What we have left is a picture in which the entire mood is hopelessly altered from what it was intended to be. Vital footage is missing for the story to have a total impact.

The Library of Congress recently discovered out-footage for a number of films, including *King Kong*. Unless this good fortune is duplicated in the case of *Klondike Annie*. Mae West's screen masterpiece will never again be seen in its entirety. The hope is somewhat diminished by the fact that Paramount Pictures sold rights and transferred negative material on its pre-1948 library to Music Corporation of America, and scrapped all excess footage years ago. The Paramount Pictures' library print is the edited version. Mae West has never owned prints of her films.

Some years before production began, Mae had written a stage play entitled *Frisco Kate*. It was a variation on the *Diamond Lil* theme. *Goin' to Town* had been rather innocuous fare; *Frisco Kate* promised to be more firmly in the West tradition. The studio bought the story and production was scheduled.

In the meantime, Marion Morgan and George B. Dowell, the writing team that had been associated with the original story for *Goin' to Town*, submitted a story set in the Klondike with a zealous missionary woman named "Soul-Savin' Annie." Mae was enthusiastic about these plot ingredients and approached Paramount to buy the screen rights. The studio was nettled. It appeared to them that all Mae was doing was trying to make writers rich. The very idea of buying an entire story for just two ideas seemed the height of folly. Only after much complaining, did Paramount finally give in.

With these added elements, Mae had more than a remake of **She Done Him Wrong**. All of the religious and spiritual questionings of her maturity, all of the moral revaluations, the clear-sighted conception of humanity amid its own foolishness and cruelty were suddenly implicit in the screenplay and were to be projected into a powerful motion picture. For mass appeal, there were songs, interesting gag lines, sets designed by A. E. Freudeman, and romance. For those who were willing or able to see it, there was much more. Perhaps without being totally cognizant of the fact, Mae was making a comment on man and organized religion.

But it's hard to say for certain with Mae. She might easily have intended every moment. No one knows the private Mae or has written about her. The public image is her life-work. When asked why she always insisted on subjects in her films likely to inspire heated discussion, like sex or, in the case of **Klondike Annie**, religion and sex, Mae answered, "All I have ever wanted to do is entertain people, make them laugh so hard they forget they'd like to cry." Somehow it doesn't sound like the kind of comment a sex-goddess would make.

It might be that, try as she would, Mae's biggest problem working in pictures was getting the public over their notion of Mae West. Every time she tried to say something profound, and in **Klondike Annie** she's being as serious as Chaplin ever was in **Modern Times** (United Artists, 1935), the public threw it right back at her, calling it "typical" Mae West. Should she deviate even slightly from the role of Mae West, in whose image she built a successful career and earned a fortune, she was criticized almost as much as she was for being Mae West. Her masterfully managed career didn't optimally allow her to show how intelligent she was.

Success can be imprisoning. In Mae's situation, it might prove disastrous, nearly as disastrous as it became for Chaplin. When you tell people the truth, or when you tell them what they don't want to hear, they can be expected to react. There is an unconscious resentment that builds up, what Freud called an unwillingness to know. In Chaplin's case, it forced him out of the United States; it sent Dashiell Hammett to prison; for Mae it shortened her time in pictures and made her last entries disappointing.

The *Hollywood Reporter* said of **Klondike Annie** on 5 February 1936: "It takes La West back to the Nineties. . . . Unlike previous West pictures, situations rather than lines offend. One scene is particularly distasteful. This is where Mae changes clothes with the dead Sister. It is unnecessary to show the flash of the dead woman with her hair curled and dressed in flimsies." The scene *was* taken out.

In the *Fox West Coast Bulletin* for 29 February 1936, a reviewer commented: " . . . The situation she creates in the Settlement House will not meet with the approval of any member of the Protestant churches. Even the men missionaries or settlement workers are caricatures. The picture is a direct insult to many of the good self-sacrificing men and women who enter this field of work. Not fit to be shown." What did Mae say from the pulpit that so offended them? Just this: "Any time you take religion for a joke the laugh is on you. You know, folks, I once made the mistake o' thinkin' religion was only for certain kinds of people, but I found out different. I came to realize that you don't have to wear a long face an' walk around bein' sad to be good. An' that's what I want you people to understand, here and now. I want to show you that you can think right and do right every day of your lives and still have a good time in this world."

She pauses to sing a song. Then she returns to the pulpit and sums up what life and success and suffering and knowing people has told her, in a few lines that constitute the essence of her moral sermon.

"I ain't here to blame you for what you've done. I ain't even goin' to tell you that you been doin' wrong. You know that better than I do. So, I'm leaving it up to your conscience to be on the level with yourself an' the world in everything you do. It's human nature to have a certain amount of weakness. It's an uphill fight tryin' to be good. It takes plenty of courage and spirit to play it that way. What you win in the end is worth it."

Lew Garvey said in the August 1936 issue of *Hollywood* magazine, "Insiders insist that the recent newspaper assaults on the picture **Klondike Annie** cut Mae deeply. She took personal pride in the benevolent quality written into the evangelist role. It was a stinging jolt to have her sincere interpretation of the character branded indecent."

Mae tried to change her act in **Klondike Annie**. She tried again, and for the last time really, to say something meaningful. She tried to take apart and analyze publicly the character she had been playing for years. The private Mae West was probing the public Mae West. The *Boston Transcript* of 29 February 1936 could only say: "The rolling gait, the husky tones, the words spoken through slightly parted teeth, even in the form of dialogue, are very familiar by now. There is a singular lack of variety in her acting. Not only is she the same in one part after another, but there is an unvarying sameness to her expression within a given characterization." Surprisingly, in this context, only the publication of the National Society of New England Women saw part of what Mae was about. The editorial on *Klondike Annie* said, "It has definite dramatic structure, the acting is very real, and the motivation is logical. It deals, of course, with a side of life ignored by polite society, but it is not without a note of genuine truth." But all argument is useless now; existing prints can, necessarily, tell only half the story.

The picture went through the usual series of name changes from **Frisco Kate** to **Frisco Doll**, then, with the change of locale, to **Klondike Lou**, and finally its release title of **Klondike Annie**. The songs, written especially for the picture by Gene Austin and Jimmie Johnson, were good ones. "I'm an Occidental Woman in an Oriental Mood for Love" was sung in Chinese costuming at Chan Lo's with legitimate Oriental instruments playing a jazz accompaniment. "Mr. Deep Blue Sea" was sung aboard ship with guitar. "Little Bar Butterfly" was the song between the sections of Mae's sermon.

Klondike Annie begins in Chinatown in the Nineties. Rose Carlton, the Frisco Doll, is Chan Lo's kept woman. He picked her up in the gutter, showered her with finery, and is violently jealous of her desire to free herself from his possessiveness. Chan has a dagger used through centuries to pierce the hearts of ladies who have betrayed their lords. Rose is an entertainment rage on the Barbary Coast. "Why won't you let me have gentlemen friends of my own race?" she asks Chan Lo. "Because it is written," he replies, "that there are only two perfectly good men, one dead, the other unborn."

"Which are you?" Rose responds.

Fah Wong, Rose's maid, hopes to escape with her. Vance Palmer tips Rose off that it's all set for her to board a boat bound for Alaska. Chan Lo hears of it by forcing an old Chinese woman, acting as a go-between, to confess the conspiracy. He tries to stop Rose. (Deleted is the scene,

similar to the stabbing of Russian Rita in **She Done Him Wrong**, where Rose wrestles with Chan for the knife and gorily puts him to death.) Cut directly from Rose intending to get away to her boarding the boat. Bull Brackett, the captain, falls in love with her, and Rose spends the better part of the voyage wrestling with his advances. When they put Fah Wong off at Seattle, Bull learns that the Frisco Doll is wanted for murder. Rose at last gives in to him.

At Vancouver, Sister Annie Alden comes aboard, also bound for Nome, and shares Rose's cabin. Immediately, she tries to convert the Doll. "Too many girls follow the line of least resistance," she tells Rose. "Yeah," says Rose, "but a good line is hard to resist." Does being holy mean you cannot permit yourself a normal sexual life? Annie's example would indicate that it is so. "You see," argues Annie, "I put my whole heart in my work." "So do I," Rose returns, adding: "You can lose your heart, but never lose your head." In the course of the voyage, Sister Annie falls ill, then dies. When the ship reaches Nome, the police board it in search of the fugitive. Rose, in her desperation, disguises herself in a missionary uniform and (deleted) dresses Annie up in prostitute's garb.

Rose continues the impersonation once they land, even though Bull would have her dodge the law and escape with him to the South Seas. There is no escape for Rose until she has paid back the debt she feels she owes Annie. The mission is in terrible straits, with $876 owed, starving people to feed, and the poor to care for. Rose determines to help the missionaries, especially after she hears the letter read aloud that Annie had sent from Vancouver. But she insists on doing things her own way. "You people," she tells them, "have been on the wrong track an' I'm going to steer you right. You'll never get anywhere 'cause you don't know how to wrassle the Devil. Tyin' a knot in his tail won't throw him on his back. Ya got to grab him by the horns. Ya got to know him, know his tricks. I know him. And how! I know him."

Rose sets the town on its ear and tough-talks even the dance hall queens into cooperating on Sunday nights. She packs the mission, gives her moving sermon, has hymns played set to popular tunes, and sends out her ushers for the collection, one-armed men. Jack Forrest, a Mountie, takes a shine to Annie, and later on they go sleigh riding together. A little kid

With Victor McLaglen

With Philip Reed

With Victor McLaglen

takes two dollars from Annie to keep his mouth shut to Bull. Brackett tries to pump the kid. "I gave yuh one dollar to let me know," he says. "Yeah," says the kid, "but she gave me two dollars to keep my mouth shut." "I'll give yuh three dollars to tell." He does. "She went skating with Brother Bowser," the kid affirms, pocketing the money. Brackett bursts into laughter. "Now," interrupts the kid, "for five dollars, I'll tell what she really did."

Brackett goes to the Doll's room to have it out with her. Forrest overhears their conversation and, upon Brackett's departure, enters and tells Rose he's heard everything. But, he assures her, it doesn't matter. He loves her anyway. He will sacrifice his career if only he can have her. Rose can't let him do that. She has been trying to do the right thing. Ruining Forrest's career would be the wrong thing. She gets back into her Frisco Doll togs, shocking Brother Bowser and the others, and says she's leaving them, thousands richer. All she asks is that they build a bigger place and call it Sister Annie Alden's Settlement House.

Once more on Bull's boat, she tells him she's innocent of the murder charge and she's going back to Frisco to prove it. He's not keen on the idea, but acquiesces. "Why," he says, "if I thought I'd lose yuh, I'd croak yuh." "Bull," says Rose, pulling him down on top of her, "ya ain't no oil paintin', but you're a fascinatin' monster."

Marion Davies, Hearst's good friend, is reputed to have attended the Hollywood premier of *Klondike Annie* and remarked afterward that she enjoyed the picture, thought Mae had never looked lovelier, and wondered over "Pop's" indignation. Hearst wasn't the only hypocrite who attacked the film. It is a tragedy that it had to be mutilated. But in what remains we have not only good Mae West, but can see the framework, at least, of the serious artist, an accomplished woman who tried to rise above her career image and touch the human heart. It is Mae's finest moment before the camera. After it, she gave up entirely trying to beat the censors. Maybe she even despaired. Never again did she come close to the depth of feeling and dark insight of *Klondike Annie.*

With Lucille Gleason

With Lyle Talbot

(Note: The picture was released on 13 November 1936. It was given a rating of "B" by the recently formed Legion of Decency, which meant "morally objectionable in part for all." Production began on 10 August 1936 and was finished by September.)

Current owner world rights: Music Corporation of America
Prints of this film may be rented for home or film society exhibition from: UNIVERSAL SIXTEEN, 425 N. MICHIGAN AVENUE, CHICAGO, ILLINOIS 60611

Among Mae West's films for Paramount release, **Go West, Young Man** has been most obscured by the passage of time. Perhaps it is just as well. It is her weakest film from the Thirties and today seems overlong, occasionally dull. Some parts of it retain their interest.

Ernst Lubitsch, whom Mary Pickford imported to this country to direct her, had an American career of varying success. Paramount made him production head of the West Coast studio in 1936. Mae didn't like him.

Emanuel Cohen decided to revamp Major Pictures as an independent producing company. Paramount would continue to distribute his films and he would have use of the Marathon Street facilities and their contract players, but Cohen's company would finance and participate to fifty percent in subsequent revenues. What was really different about all this was Cohen's self-financing.

Go West, Young Man

Paramount, 1936
Running time: 82 minutes

Producer   Emanuel Cohen
Producing company   Major Pictures
Releasing company   Paramount Pictures
Director   Henry Hathaway
Based on play by   Lawrence Riley
Play presented by   Brock Pemberton & Antoinette Perry
Screenplay   Mae West
Music   Arthur Johnston
Lyrics   John Burke
Musical director   George Stoll
Gowns   Irene Jones
Art director   Wiard Ihnen
Photography   Karl Struss, A.S.C.
Film editor   Ray Curtiss
Sound Engineer   Hugo Grenzbach

CAST

Mavis Arden   Mae West
Morgan   Warren William
Bud Norton   Randolph Scott
Mrs. Struthers   Alice Brady
Aunt Kate   Elizabeth Patterson
Francis X. Harrigan   Lyle Talbot
Gladys   Isabel Jewell
Joyce   Margaret Perry
Professor Rigby   Etienne Giradot
Clyde   Maynard Holmes
Chauffeur   John Indrisano
Maid   Alice Ardell
Nicodemus   Nicodemus Stewart
Master of Ceremonies   Charles Irwin
Andy Kelton   Walter Walker
In Drifting Lady:
Rico   Jack LaRue
Philip   G.P. Huntley, Jr.
Officer   Robert Baikoff
Xavier Cugat   Himself
Extra   Eddie Dunn
Reporter   Dick Elliott
Bumpkin   Si Jenks

With director Henry Hathaway

He wanted freedom to produce films as he saw fit and not be subject to Lubitsch.

Mae had two uncompleted films on her contract which Cohen took over personally; they became *Go West, Young Man* and *Every Day's a Holiday*. Neither was especially lucrative, *Every Day's a Holiday* dying a sudden, unexpected, and undeserved death at the box office. The reasons behind their failure, while complex, simplify in principle to one word: censorship. The rising tide of moral indignation was reaching overwhelming proportions. Mae was so stringently restricted that even an adult rating was now contingent, as in the case of *Every Day's a Holiday*, upon striking inoffensive lines. Her delivery itself was under fire. Mae resisted, but the pressure was wearing her down.

Forced to abandon what had been the staple of her popularity, Mae's films now assumed more than ever the appearance of a one-woman cavalcade; unlike *Belle of the Nineties*, they had strong plots, but anemic dialogues. Mae tried to conceive funny situations, rather than humorous commentaries on life. If the later films prove anything, it's the fact that Mae's forte was never situation comedy. She needed her brash, uninhibited satire.

Emanuel Cohen was impressed by the long Broadway run of Lawrence Riley's stage play *Personal Appearance*, in which Gladys George portrayed a star forbidden by contract to marry for a period of five years. The comedy came about through her amorous dalliances; the tragedy resulted from the repressive actions of her press agent, whom she finally chucks.

Cohen negotiated the screen rights and wanted it to form the basis for Mae's first film under the new arrangement. Mae rewrote the story to suit herself. She had been making tours with her films for years. It was this experience from which she drew in working out her screenplay. However, since the title of the stage work might be misleading to movie patrons, it was altered to one more intimately connected with her. Whatever help the Riley success might have given the film, the play on words once spoken by Horace Greeley didn't assist at the box office.

"I've been taking motion pictures seriously," Mae told Frederick James Smith in an interview in *Screen Book* magazine for May 1933. "When I saw myself in *Night After Night* I said, Mae, you photograph too heavy. The camera adds ten pounds to you, but even so, I wasn't right. I took off weight where I needed it. Here and here. I look better in *She Done Him Wrong*. Don't tell me you think I ought to reduce. I think that the pictures are all wrong in the way they feature starved ingenues. You know, the flat-chested girls you see on the screen. If I know men, I know . . . they don't care for scrawny girls. They want something to get their hands on when they grab a girl. Or am I wrong? Continued reducing makes the Hollywood girls look like those neediest cases you hear about. Pained faces, sharp shoulders, knobby knees, terrible spaces between their legs. So flat you can't tell which way they're going."

In July 1937, *Hollywood* magazine compared Mae's measurements with those of Venus de Milo. "Venus de Milo: bust, 34¾ inches; waist, 28½ inches; hips, 36 inches; middle thigh, 19½ inches; calf, 13½ inches; ankle, 8½ inches. Mae West: bust, 35 inches; waist, 27½ inches; hips, 36 inches; middle thigh, 19½ inches; calf, 13 inches; ankle, 8¼ inches."

The *Motion Picture Herald*, one of the most avidly read trade magazines, said of *Go West, Young Man* and Mae's performance in it on 14 November 1936: "She sings rather pitifully, two songs and virtually throughout the picture undulates and weaves, giving visual as well as verbal point to the tiresome series of suggestive lines. Incidentally, the fight with obesity seems to be getting her down."

Paramount's publicity department regularly touched up all Mae West photos, slimming and streamlining her. *Photoplay* featured an article on Mae, telling how she had to drink several glasses of milk a day to keep her weight up. Mae was sensitive on the subject. In November 1933, *Screen Book* magazine quoted her as saying, "You can bet clothes make the woman—and there isn't enough to these skimpy things the girls have been wearing to do 'em much good! I don't see why there can't be modified versions of Lady Lou's costumes, especially for the evening. They won't kill the 1933 girl any more than they did the 1890 belle. She ought to be able to carry them as well as her mother did. Oh, I don't mean to go back into all that tight corseting. Heaven knows, I do not blame women for fighting stays. But the big hats, the voluminous furs, the wide-spreading skirts, and the *curves*—if you think they don't make a woman attractive just ask any man. Now understand me, I do not mean any sudden swelling out. To the bulging bosom and hips I say no! To graceful curves, yes. There is no use kidding ourselves: We're feminine and such things as bosoms do exist

With Xavier Cugat and his Orchestra

and they have come back. Flat chests are as taboo and outdated as yesterday's paper." She was prophetic, and the age of the flapper passed.

"No prescribed set of rules restrict the pleasure-loving lady of the cinema," Lew Garvey reported in the article which compared Mae and Venus de Milo. "She eats when she is hungry—and when she's hungry she eats plenty."

While this debate was continuing, religious fanatics and guardians of public morals lined up their broadsides. The California Congress of Parents and Teachers said of **Go West, Young Man**, "It is destructive of ethical standards, somewhat demoralizing, and totally lacking in charm." "A burlesque on Mae West by Mae West herself," commented the Southern California Council of Federated Church Women. "The characterization is a paradox of elegance and bad grammar, of vulgar sex appeal and glamorous costuming." The General Federation of Women's Clubs didn't even leave Mae her costumes: "It is replete with sly innuendoes and daring vulgarities,

cheaply entertaining." J. P. Cunningham went further in *Commonweal* and related, "Someone has said that the sex in Mae West's newest picture is of elephantine subtlety. Vulgar would be more explicit, with the added disadvantage of establishing a new low mark in entertainment for the Mae West series."

The *New York Herald Tribune* reviewer wrote that **Go West** "displays the increasingly ample Mae West in a slipshod and tedious offering. . . . She runs through her limited repertory of acting tricks over and over again and even her efforts at innuendo are less ribald than ludicrous." The *Christian Science Monitor* said of it, "Lengthy, coarse, and not very funny. Mae West as a movie star stranded in the sticks displays her limitations."

I would be misleading the reader were I to imply that all reviews of **Go West, Young Man** were unanimous. But public dislike of Mae West was mounting in certain sectors. In **Go West**, as much as anything, Mae tried to suggest that she was not the characters she had played on the screen,

127

and hence the attempt at self-parody. Most of her violent detractors took it as just another Westian thrust at virginity, purity, and innocence. The coming war, I think, dispelled a lot of this stuffy hypocrisy and foolishness, so that now Westian standards seem almost inanely conventional. If the hysteria and viciousness appear quaint today, they were nevertheless very real then, building into a crescendo that erupted after the Bergen-McCarthy broadcast.

The *New York Times* remarked, "Generally speaking, *Personal Appearance* has lost little in Miss West's edition. . . . The salty idiom and the haughty malapropisms that punctuated the stage piece have been retained wherever they could be got by the censors, and there is something to be said for Miss West's presentation of these features . . . the supporting cast is uniformly excellent. . . ." *Variety* said, "No Mae West picture has been more Westful, or more zestful. It is earthy, erotic, pungent . . . the picture doesn't overstep the bounds of offensiveness within the censorial permissions."

Go West, Young Man was Henry Hathaway's first comedy. He had directed Randolph Scott previously in Paramount's Zane Grey series. It was a wholly competent cast. Lyle Talbot handed in a fine performance as the erstwhile politician Francis X. Harrigan, who was never seen in the play, while Etienne Giradot made a good Professor Rigby. Nicodemus Stewart is a trifle exasperating, playing

With Randolph Scott

Elizabeth Patterson, Isabel Jewell, Alice Brady, and Warren William

a stupid Negro. Isabel Jewell is splendid as a star-struck hick. Warren William, a recent Paramount addition from Warner Bros., carries the show, even after all these years, as the press agent. Karl Struss once more managed some exceptional portrait photography of Mae.

The story opens to a film within the film, a packed theatre avidly viewing the latest Mavis Arden celluloid romance. The device is too heavy-handed in its presentation to be very amusing. "I hate liars!" Mae's screen character says. "No man can support a wife an' me at the same time." The screen character proceeds to ditch a succession of amorous males.

Morgan, Mavis's press agent, introduces her in person to the audience at the conclusion of the picture. The malapropisms begin with Mavis's confusion as to whether she works for Super Fine Pictures or Stupifyin' Pictures. She tells the audience that she longs for a simple life in an Italian villa, preferably located in Hollywood.

It is Morgan's job to keep Mavis from all

129

With Jack Perrin, Warren William, Lee Shumway and Lyle Talbot

With Randolph Scott

With Warren William

emotional entanglements with men. She goes out on a date with a Washington politician, Harrigan, who is an old friend of hers. Morgan subverts their quiet dinner by having it invaded by a throng of reporters. Mavis's motto is "A thrill a day keeps the chill away." Mavis comes out, during the subsequent interview, in favor of supportive matrimony, thinking it should be subsidized by the Government. Harrigan, shaking in his boots over possible repercussions, winds up amazed at the positive effusions from the electorate. Mavis rewards Morgan with a custard pie in the face as she leaves the nightclub.

For *Go West*, Mae could update her fashions, due to its contemporary setting. She also cast her Rolls-Royce. The car breaks down while en route to Harrisburg. Mavis and Morgan put up at Mrs. Struthers's Haven. A discussion is going on among the women about Mavis Arden and her new picture, *Drifting Lady*. Aunt Kate tells of the women of her youth. "They had 'it' all right, but they didn't photograph it and put it to music." Mrs. Struthers is a snob reduced to running a boarding house.

Mavis's arrival sets off a small riot. "In my time," Aunt Kate says, "women with hair like that didn't come outside in the daylight." Mavis comments to Morgan about her producer, A. K. Greenfield, "A. K. was right when he said we was makin' pictures for a lot of morons." Mavis's longing to get on to Harrisburg evaporates when she observes Randolph Scott's large and sinewy muscles.

Isabel Jewell waylays Morgan and performs for him a wretched impersonation of Marlene Dietrich. Mavis in the interim toddles out to Scott's workshop. He wants to demonstrate his sound reproduction invention; Mavis is on the make. She strolls with him back toward the house, flopping in a haystack on the way. She holds out her arms and invites Scott to join her. Morgan and her fans among the local yokels catch up to her just in time and she spends the remainder of the afternoon signing autographs.

Joyce, Scott's girlfriend, has a fight with him over Mavis. Professor Rigby is also outraged by Mavis's behavior and is intent upon telling the whole story to a scandal sheet. Mavis enjoins Morgan to prevent him.

   Morgan: How can I stop him?
   Mavis: Steal his pants.

Morgan instead undertakes to persuade the professor that Mavis wants him to appear in her next picture, whereupon he gives forth with Hamlet's soliloquy.

Harrigan attempts to telephone Mavis, overhears some talk about kidnapping, and assumes she is the victim. Mavis is busy working on Scott, who is busy on his invention. She would like to take them both to Hollywood. Mavis sings a sultry song, and they dance together. Isabel Jewell, hearing about the kidnaping on a radio news broadcast, believes Morgan to be the culprit and together with her dimwitted boyfriend goes off to notify the police. Aunt Kate has some sage advice for Joyce in her competition with Mavis: "If this woman's got something that's taken him away, find out what it is and add something to it." Aunt Kate then goes down to interrupt the lovers by switching on the living room radio. "It isn't often we have any night life in this house," she says.

"You don't give it a chance to develop," Mavis responds.

To no avail, Aunt Kate insists Morgan break up the affair, claiming that Mavis has stolen Scott's heart and his invention too. Morgan has a talk with Mavis, producing a baby sweater and commenting that it is a present for Joyce who, supposedly, is pregnant by Scott. Marvis, in turn, tells Scott that everything is off. She falls back on the hackneyed dialogue from *Drifting Lady* in telling him. When later she learns that Joyce isn't pregnant, she knocks Morgan unconscious just as an envoy of policemen arrives to arrest him for kidnaping her. Morgan, when he comes to, tells Mavis where she can go. "I liked you 'cause I thought you had some feeling," he says. "But when you didn't, I liked you even more." She extricates him from the law, and at the fade is feeling his muscles. "Men are my life," she murmurs. "A. K. shall hear of this," Morgan says, drawing her to him. "I promise you."

If there is any criticism to be levelled at Mae West for her work in *Go West*, it is that her humor suffers from the limitations placed upon it. She enjoyed a fine supporting cast, technical and otherwise, but comedy at her expense, as opposed to being at the expense of others, and particularly comedy which did not reflect her in a sympathetic light, hurt her more than it helped. The plot placed her in what was an artificial and unnatural position that begged the viewer's credibility. Mavis Arden was too much Mae West to be exposed as a shallow Hollywood luminary and vamp, just as Mae was too much Mavis Arden, in her characterization, to wrench from the role the necessary freewheeling satire she especially requires. As a consequence, *Go West, Young Man* emerged as an entertaining but somehow troubling and dissatisfying film.

Interlude: Mae West On Radio

As Christmas 1937 approached, the United States was in the midst of the recession that replaced the Depression. Bureaucracy had clamped its fingers around the throat of the nation and the long, gasping, and so far *losing* battle on the part of Americans to preserve their civil liberties and their constitutional freedoms had begun in earnest. Everywhere the tentacles of government entwined the governed.

On the brighter side, Louis B. Mayer, vice president of Metro-Goldwyn-Mayer, busied himself with preparations for his network broadcast party for the cast of *Rosalie.* According to four hundred radio editors polled by the *Motion Picture Daily,* Charlie McCarthy, Edgar Bergen's dummy, beat out previous champion Jack Benny as radio's most popular entertainer. The charter members of the Benevolent Order of Santa Clauses were about to convene in Brooklyn, where they would vote Mae West and Shirley Temple as a tie for first place among favorite motion picture stars. Emanuel Cohen and Paramount were on the verge of releasing Mae's new million-dollar picture, *Every Day's a Holiday.* And on Sunday evening, 12 December 1937, Mae West was scheduled to appear on the Chase & Sanborn Hour, hosted by Edgar Bergen and Charlie McCarthy.

Mae wanted to perform a scene from her new film, but the writers at J. Walter Thompson, Chase & Sanborn's advertising agency, had a better idea: a breakfast skit over hot C & S coffee, with Mae and regular master of ceremonies Don Ameche doing an Adam and Eve satire. Charlie, as the snake, would be the uninvited guest. Mae claimed afterwards that she had scarcely looked at the script. Her delivery of lines, so filled with mistakes and indirections, would bear her out. Cohen encouraged the appearance. Little did he know . . .

No one has heard this broadcast since. Fred Allen called the radio comedian's fate a "treadmill to oblivion," because heard once, his humor is henceforth no more than a memory. So it would be now were it not, in this instance, for the noted critic of American musicals, Miles Kreuger. Several years ago, at a dull party, he happened to read an article of mine and called me from New York; it was long distance to Milwaukee, and it cost a fortune. In the course of our conversation he mentioned that he had a great many historic radio broadcasts, air checks recorded on acetate, and subsequently transferred by him to magnetic tape. I asked him if he had Mae West's Chase & Sanborn adventure, and, when he said that he had, I asked him for a copy of it. His kindness to me has made my comments below possible.

The show opened with Ameche talking about the odds of Charlie succumbing to Mae's charms.

Ameche: Why do you say it's a tough fight?
Charlie: Well, my opponent's in great form.

Mae was introduced. After a few interchanges, she said, "Charlie, why don't you walk out on Bergen? What's holdin' yuh?"

"Well," Charlie responded, "He is."
Then:

Charlie: You'd better tell him, Mae.
Mae: All right, if yuh wanna know, he did come up to see me.
Bergen: Oh, he did. And what was he doing up there?
Mae: Well, Charlie came up an' I showed him my etchings. *(Pause. The program is cut off the air. It returns to raucous laughter.)*
Mae: An' he showed me his stamp collection.
Charlie: There you have it, Bergen, there you have it.
Bergen: Yes, so that's all there was to it . . . etchings and a stamp collection?
Charlie: *(aside, chuckling)* Haha, he's so naive!

"It looks bad, Bergen.
Yes, it looks bad."
   —Charlie McCarthy

After another short interchange, Mae commented testily: "I thought you were gonna have a nice long talk Tuesday night at my apartment. Where did you go when the doorbell rang?"

Charlie: Well, I tried to hide in your clothes closet, but two guys kicked me out. (*Laughter*) So, I went out the back door.
Mae: Don't tell me you went down . . . uh, out the French windows? I'm on the third floor, y' know.
Charlie: Oh, so that's what it was, the French windows, huh? I was gonna say you were pretty skimpy with those back steps. (*Laughter*)

What proved to be the most amusing moments of the show took this form:

Charlie: Could you even like Mr. Bergen?
Mae: Ah, Mr. Bergen. He's very sweet. In fact, he's a right guy. Confidentially, yuh'll have to show me a man I don't like.
Charlie: That's swell! Bergen's your man. You know, he can be *had.*
Mae: On second thought, I'm liable to take him away from yuh. Then what'll yuh say?
Charlie: Well, if you take Bergen away, I'm speechless. (*Laughter*)
Mae: Why don't you come up . . . uh, home with me now, honey? I'll let yuh play in my woodpile. (*Laughter*)
Charlie: Well, I'm not feeling so well tonight. I've been feeling nervous lately. I think I'm gonna have a nervous breakdown. Whuup! There I go.
Mae: So, good-time Charlie's gonna play hard to get. Well, yuh can't kid me. You're afraid of women. Your Casanova stuff is just a front, a false front.
Charlie: Not so loud, Mae, not so loud! All my girlfriends are listening.
Mae: Oh, yeah! You're all wood and a yard long . . .
Charlie: (*weakly*) Yeah.
Mae: Yuh weren't so nervous and backward when yuh came up to see me at my apartment. In fact, yuh didn't need any encouragement to kiss me.
Charlie: Did I do that?
Mae: Why, yuh certainly did. I got marks to prove it. (*Snickering from audience*) An' splinters, too. (*Laughter*)

The Adam and Eve skit was nothing special.

Mae did ask Ameche to "try this apple sometime, honey," but it undoubtedly was the biblical source more than anything else that some people found offensive. The furor following the broadcast was all out of proportion to what had been on the air. It surprised everyone, not the least of whom was Mae. Frank R. McNinch, whom President Roosevelt had transferred from the Federal Power Commission to "clean up radio" by bossing the Federal Communications Commission, informed NBC president Lenox R. Lohr that protests claimed the broadcast was "profane," "obscene," "dirty," "sexy," and "insulting to the American public."

Martin Quigley of the *Motion Picture Herald* rallied the industry attack. "Evidence indicates they sent for her," he wrote. "She was bought, not sold. . . . A clear-eyed examination of the facts will disclose a daughter of a Brooklyn prizefighter . . . crystallized . . . into . . . a symbolism of attainable sex, garnished with the ostrich plumes of the red plush parlor period. . . . Mae West got the biggest cocktail hour and smoking compartment line of word-of-mouth publicity in the annals of commercialized fame and the more she got talked about, the more photographs of her in variant degrees of deciduousness appeared in the public prints, the less she was acceptable to the family-communal motion picture audience." Of the broadcast, he said: "No religious issue was or is involved. Indecency is indecency in anybody's religion, and it is still indecency even if one has no religion." Now that's saying a lot!

The guardians of public morals were certain, and certitude has never known restraint in these matters. The *New York Sun* commented, "On any other day of the week the skit would have justified the severest criticism from the standpoint of good taste, but on Sunday such a broadcast represents the all-time low in radio. The most charitable explanation is that the producers were mesmerized by the reputed glamour of the entertainer."

It wasn't long before legislators twisted indignation into a platform advocating more governmental control of the governed. William P. Connery, Jr., Democrat of Massachusetts, promised the nation a bill to investigate radio. He demanded that KFI, the Hollywood NBC station where the show originated, have its license revoked. In a letter to McNinch, the congressman charged that the program "violated the sensibilities of even those who are familiar with the burlesquing of historical [*sic*] events." Donald L. O'Toole, Democrat of New York, seconded Connery, adding, "If a company has not sufficient sense not to allow such a program, then censorship must be exercised."

An anti-Mae West faction became articulate when Walter Vincent, chairman of the Motion Picture Theatre Owners committee to study box-office/radio relations was joined by critics like Ashton Stevens of the *Chicago American*, a Hearst paper, Lester Gottlieb of Mutual Broadcasting, an NBC rival, and others in condemning Mae and the program.

NBC controlled fifteen stations and altogether had fifty-nine affiliates that carried the broadcast. KFI was one of their strongest stations with direct access to Hollywood talent. Representative W. D. McFarlane of Texas declared that RCA's domination of RKO Radio Pictures, its phonograph company, Victor Records, and the National Broadcasting Company constituted a monopoly. McNinch drafted a letter to NBC president Lohr and advised him that "Section 326 of the Federal Communications Act of 1934 provides that no person shall utter any obscene, indecent, or profane language by means of radio communications. This Commission is charged by law with the enforcement of that provision." The writers of the script insisted that the famous Westian "inflections" might have prompted unintended meanings over the airwaves. If so, they gave her more than a little help.

The Catholics outdid the Protestants in their outrage. Reverend Dr. Maurice S. Sheehy of Catholic University termed the show "the most indecent, scurrilous, and religiously irreverent program that it has ever been my misfortune to hear. Under the direction of a committee of Bishops, the Legion of Decency has done much to raise the moral standards of the movies." He suggested the Legion branch out into radio.

Stanley Resor, president of the J. Walter Thompson Co., which with the help of behaviorist psychologists had determined that red boxes exert a sexual attraction on women buyers, apologized for the Adam and Eve skit in a letter to Lohr at NBC. "On behalf of our client, Chase & Sanborn, we wish to express our deepest regret that the program . . . gave offense to anyone. . . . The script of this feature of the broadcast was our responsibility. It was a mistake, and we can assure the public at large that the same mistake will not be made again."

Lohr replied, in part, "We share with you the regret you express as we share also the responsibility in this incident. Our interests are entirely mutual in striving to give the American public the type of wholesome entertainment which it wants, and which it has every right to expect." Together the two of them sounded like Japanese diplomats excusing the bombing of Shanghai.

Chase & Sanborn said over the air, in the voice of announcer Ronald Drake, and not Don Ameche, "It has been brought to the attention of the sponsors of this program that a skit on it last Sunday offended the religious sensibilities of our listeners. Our hope is to make each and every hour spent with us both entertaining and edifying."

All mention of Mae West, *any* use of her name, was prohibited on radio, a gratuitous act of self-regulation. Miss West was unavailable for comment. Paramount and Emanuel Cohen made a joint announcement that they had nothing whatsoever, either individually or collectively, to do with the broadcast. *Every Day's a Holiday* ended their association with Mae West.

McNinch reported the Commission's findings in this fashion: "A clear recognition of the social, civic, and moral responsibility for the effect upon listeners of all classes and ages requires such a high

standard for programs as would insure against features that are suggestive; vulgar, immoral, or of such character as may be offensive to the great mass of right-thinking, clean-minded American citizens."

By the time Mae West came to write her autobiography, she was still smarting from the uproar, and disclaimed any real involvement. The publicity photos released at the time with Charlie and Mae presumably at her apartment at least indicate that she was being exploited. For all of the freedom of our present attitudes toward most of what Mae says in her films, and even the relative liberation of motion pictures themselves, radio and television censorship has become increasingly constricted. I think this is probably due to the amount of control Government can exercise over such programming through the Federal Communications Commission. They haven't found

a way to do it yet to book publishing, movies, and magazines.

It is one of the most tragic ironies of our era that there are some cities where you dare not walk the streets, even around your own block, after ten at night; and there are cities where you can be jailed as an ordinary citizen should you refuse to identify yourself. When you are indoors, you are assured that your morals shall not be subverted through the communication media. Minorities actually feel they can dictate what popular images will be, and Government supports them in their efforts. Just so, politicians can still be heard to complain that insufficient vigilance exists and more must yet be done. It is almost as if, the clearer the public mind, the more narrow the minds of the ruling forces. It is strange.

Every Day's A Holiday

Paramount, 1938
Running time: 80 minutes.

Producer   Emanuel Cohen
Producing company   Major Pictures
Releasing Company   Paramount Pictures
Director   A. Edward Sutherland
Assistant director   Earl Rettig
Production manager   Joe Nadel
Screenplay   Mae West
Musical director   LeRoy Prinz
Arrangements   Leo Shuken
Songs: "Fifi" and "Little Butterfly"   Sam Coslow
       "Every Day's A Holiday"   Sam Coslow & Barry Trivers
       "Jubilee"   Hoagy Carmichael & Stanley Adams
Gowns by   Schiaparelli
Art director   Wiard Ihnen
Wardrobe   Basia Bassett
Photography   Karl Struss, A.S.C.
Special photographic effects   Gordon Hennings, A.S.C.
Film editor   Ray Curtiss
Sound engineer   Hugo Grenzbach

CAST

Peaches O'Day   Mae West
Madamoiselle Fifi   Mae West
Captain Jim McCarey   Edmund Lowe
Larmuadou Graves   Charles Butterworth
Van Reigble Van Pelter Van Doon, III   Charles Winninger
Nifty Bailey   Walter Catlett
Honest John Quade   Lloyd Nolan
Band Leader   Louis Armstrong
George Rector   Himself
Fritz Krausmeyer   Herman Bing
Trigger Mike   Roger Imhoff
Cabby   Chester Conklin
Danny the Dip   Lucian Prival
Assistant police commissioner   Adrian Morris
Henchman   Francis McDonald
Henchman   John Indrisano
Quartet   Irving Bacon, Allan Rogers, Otto Fries, John "Skins" Miller
Bar patron   Dick Elliot
Bartender   James C. Morton
Cop at store window   Edgar Dearing
Extra   Johnny Arthur
Extra   William Austin

As Mademoiselle Fifi

With Emanuel Cohen, head of Major Pictures

*(Note: **Every Day's a Holiday** was placed into general theatrical release on 14 January 1938. For better or worse, it was Mae West's last Paramount picture, and it was presented by Adolph Zukor, whose company, during one of its periodic crises facing ruin, she saved, and like those who had saved it before and after her, she went on to other things, while Paramount stayed. Production began on 11 October and concluded shortly before Miss West appeared on the Chase & Sanborn Hour.)*

At Christmastime 1937, Walt Disney released his all-color cartoon feature **Snow White and the Seven Dwarfs** through the RKO exchanges. It met with immediate acceptance at the box office while other pictures slumped. Mae commented, "The only picture to make money recently was **Snow White and the Seven Dwarfs**, and that would have made twice as much if they had let me play Snow White."

Every Day's a Holiday cost nearly a million dollars, and was a much stronger film than **Go West, Young Man.** It had the most skilled supporting talent of any of Mae's films, which is saying a lot. In her autobiography, Mae quotes Sheila Graham as thinking **Every Day's a Holiday** superior to **She Done Him Wrong.** It was certainly a minority viewpoint. *The New York Times* review by Frank S. Nugent stated, "Sex ain't what it used to be, or maybe Miss West isn't. Anyway, it requires more indulgence than we can muster on short notice to give her more than credit for an old Westian try. But she died game." "Miss West goes, as usual," Nugent added, "armed with her Parthian shots, among which are several duds."

Mae had had the idea to do a film based on the life of Catherine the Great, which notion was to become an obsession over the next several years. Cohen had other plans. He had a great many high-budget sets on the Paramount lot he wanted to use, including an exact replica of Rector's restaurant from the turn of the century period. He had Sam Coslow, who would work on Disney's **Song of the South,** to do the musical numbers. And he had a story idea of his own. Mae gave him her customary opposition, but she didn't win out.

Edward Sutherland was scheduled to direct. He sat in on Sam Coslow's musical session with Mae and Cohen. Coslow had a little ditty he called "Madamoiselle Fifi," about a New York city girl who went to Paris, learned French ways, and returned an entertainment triumph to American shores. Mae liked the song, but the producer and director did not. It prompted her to devise a wholly new scenario.

Mae's habit of dictating story material when the inspiration first came to her, as in the writing of **The Constant Sinner,** held true in this instance. Cohen summoned a stenographer and within an hour and a half Mae had the plot worked out, down to the minor incidents. It managed to incorporate all of Cohen's sets. It altered Mae's screen character from siren to confidence woman with strong loyalties and a sense of fair play in contrast to the political corruption and shady machinations of the self-righteous. For the first time on screen, Mae wore a dark-colored coiffure. Sexual suggestion was at an all-time low. But the Bergen-McCarthy broadcast focused public indignation and killed **Every Day's a Holiday** in the process.

"Social values censurable," wrote the *American Legion Auxiliary*, "the picture is a slap at the ethics of the police and makes a heroine of a thief." The East Coast Preview Committee remarked, "Mae West has little to offer in the way of acting and in spite of seemingly innocuous lines, her posturings are definitely vulgar."

The Hays Office clamped down so hard on Mae that they excised a line like, "I wouldn't even lift my veil for that guy." No one at the Southern California Council of Federated Church Women was aware of it. Their review summarized: "A typical Mae West picture, with the usual disgusting, suggestive dialogue and action ridiculing any attempt at reform in public officialdom. Vulgar and offensive."

The *Hollywood Spectator* at least acknowledged the truth: "Coming to the screens of the country while the public is still discussing the lack of good taste by Mae West in her radio broadcast a week ago last Sunday, I am afraid **Every Day's a Holiday** will encounter tough going. . . . It is going to be met with a barrage of critical comment which the others escaped."

Variety was friendly: "By whatever standard posterity judges the acting career of Mae West, it never shall be said that she was ever dull. And her new film is a lively, innocuously bawdy and rowdy entertainment, more typical of the star of **She Done Him Wrong** than her other recent vehicles." *Boxoffice* gave **Every Day's a Holiday** a family rating and said in part that the "picture emerges as a robust and vigorous comedy, sure to please her many fans as well as anything she has ever made and endowed with the qualities to win her new admirers since it avoids to a large degree the suggestive innuendoes which have heretofore been identified with her screen appearances." And then *Boxoffice* made a false prediction, unaware of the virulence of the crusade against her: "Whether the controversy which followed her recent air appearance will help or hinder the picture's box-office record is a moot question; but it is reasonable to assume that, if the public runs true to form, it should prove an asset." It didn't. **Every**

With Restaurateur George Rector

Day's a Holiday was the first Mae West vehicle not to make money.

The picture begins on New Year's Eve 1899 with an extravagant production of the song, "Little Butterfly," accompanied by brilliant choreography. Mae's role is that of a confidence woman named Peaches O'Day who earns her living selling the Brooklyn Bridge to suckers. (When Mae was a little girl, the boys called her "Peaches" as a nickname.) John Quade is a police inspector "so crooked he uses a corkscrew for a ruler." Captain Jim McCarey is an honest cop, and while he tries to keep Peaches honest, he doesn't serve a warrant on her, realizing that Quade has got interests unrelated to justice in her case.

Peaches mistakes Graves, Van Doon's butler, for Van Doon himself, and the two of them decide to spend the evening together. Chester Conklin shows up in an amusing scene as a cabby. Out on her date with Graves, the butler gets drunk and Peaches goes shopping with a glass-cutter, entering a department store display window and donning a sumptuous gown and furs.

Louis Armstrong leading the parade

With Edmund Lowe

> *Graves:* Hasn't this a slight touch of larcency?
> *Peaches:* Larceny, nothin'! You'll send 'em a check in the morning.

The Rector's set proved magnificent. When Peaches arrives, she meets Nifty Bailey, who wants her to star in his new review. Peaches is also introduced to the real Van Doon, who, for the evening, is willing to accept his erstwhile butler on an equal footing. After helping bring in the New Year, Peaches stops next day to visit Nifty. McCarey shows up with twenty-five warrants for her arrest.

> *Peaches:* This reflects on my honesty.
> *Bailey:* Have you ever heard it questioned?
> *Peaches:* I never even heard it mentioned.

Bailey undertakes to smuggle Peaches out of the city on a boat bound for Boston, and McCarey helps him to do it. Peaches returns in a brunette wig as the French sensation Madamoiselle Fifi, becoming the headliner in Nifty's show. Quade is running for mayor. Looking out of his office window, Quade sees his billboard campaign poster being covered up with an announcement of the show's opening. He cons Bailey out of some free tickets and even McCarey gets a ticket from the resplendent Nifty.

With Charles Butterworth and Charles Winninger

Quade is overwhelmed by Madamoiselle Fifi's performance and wants to take up with her. She pretends to be indisposed. Quade is irked, "An' me sending 'er orchids at $25 a smell!" Despite the fact that the theatre is quite new, Quade orders McCarey to close it up as a firetrap. Quade grows insistent when McCarey refuses, and McCarey resigns. McCarey once interceded for Peaches when she sold the Brooklyn Bridge to a German immigrant by the name of Fritz Krausmeyer by paying him back the $200 out of his own pocket.

Peaches, as Fifi, visits Quade at his office and burns the file containing her police record. Quade subsequently exposes her disguise, but he is without evidence capable of convicting her. Peaches nominates McCarey for mayor on the reform ticket.

> *Bailey:* How do you know McCarey will make a good mayor?
> *Peaches:* That's one guy you can't go wrong with. I found that out.

Louis Armstrong was signed for musical support. He leads a McCarey rally in a street sweeper's guise, blowing his trumpet. "Laugh, sing, and vote," Peaches urges the crowd. Fritz Krausmeyer overhears Quade planning McCarey's

With Edmund Lowe

With Lloyd Nolan

Top, with Charles Winninger, Weldon Hayburn, Herbert Rawlinson, Maude Eburne, Ferdinand Munier, and Charles Butterworth

murder. He tips off Peaches. She determines to have McCarey kidnaped so Quade can't get at him. The mickey backfires and knocks out Graves, Bailey, and Van Doon before it does McCarey. Quade's men come upon the scene and spirit McCarey away with them.

Election evening, McCarey is tied up, a prisoner of Danny the Dip and his gang of thugs. Peaches leads the parade for McCarey. A suspenseful moment precedes McCarey's escape, while Peaches sums up Quade's intentions, "He don't mean *what* he can do for the city, but *how* he can do this city."

McCarey is elected and the film ends happily with Quade crushed by defeat.

Every Day's a Holiday has its winning scenes, but it is scarcely as memorable as any of Mae's early Paramount pictures. Most of the vituperation against it was undeserved. *The New York Times* aptly chronicled its complaints about the picture by quoting Mae's response to McCarey's question of whether Quade had made love to her, "Well, he went through all the emotions." Something's missing. That something might best be described as passion. Even after all this time, it still comes out that way.

My Little Chickadee

Universal, 1940
Running time 7,498ft./83 minutes.

Producing company Universal Pictures
Executive Producer Lester Cowan
Director Edward Cline
Assistant director Joe McDonough
Original screenplay Mae West, W.C. Fields
Musical score Frank Skinner
Musical director Charles Previn
Song: "Willie of the Valley"
Lyrics Milton Drake
Music Ben Oakland
Photography Joseph Valentine
Art director Jack Otterson
Gowns by Vera West
Film editor Ed Curtiss
Sound engineer Bernard B. Brown

CAST

Flower Belle Lee Mae West
Cuthbert J. Twillie W.C. Fields
Jeff Badger Joseph Calleia
Masked Bandit Joseph Calleia
Wayne Carter Dick Foran
Mrs. Gideon Margaret Hamilton
Clarence George Moran
Old Man Si Jenks
Bartender James Conlon
Gene Austin Himself

Candy Russell Hall
Coco Otto Heimel
Henchman Eddie Butler
Henchman Bing Conley
Cousin Zeb Fuzzy Knight
Miss Foster Ann Nagel
Aunt Lou Ruth Donnelly
Uncle John Willard Robertson
Amos Budget Donald Meek

Sheriff William B. Davidson
Judge Addison Richards
Boy Jackie Searle
Mrs. "Pygmy" Allen Fay Adler
Woman Jan Duggan
Man Morgan Wallace
Man Wade Boteler
Clerk Harlan Briggs

Also appearing in uncredited bits or as extras:
Jeff Conlon, John Kelly, Walter McGrail, Otto Hoffmann, Billy Benedict, Delmar Watson, Chester Gan, George Melford (the director), Lita Chevret, Bud Harris, Bob McKenzie, James Morton, Joe Whitehead, Slim Gaut, Lloyd Ingraham, George Billings, Ben Hall, Charles McMurphy, Dick Rush, Hank Bell, Buster Slaven, Danny Jackson, Lane Chandler, Charles Hart, Jack Roper, Alan Bridge, Eddie Hearn, and Mark Anthony.

(Note: It is worth comment that both Mae and Bill Fields brought several members of their traditional stock companies to work in this production. For Mae, Gene Austin as her musical backup, for Fields Jimmy Conlon as a bartender. William B. Davidson from I'm No Angel is back as a sheriff. The film was released on 9 February 1940. Production began on 12 November 1939 and concluded in December.)

Current owner world rights: Music Corporation of America
Prints of this film may be rented for home or film society exhibition from: Universal Sixteen, 425 N. Michigan Avenue, Chicago, Illinois 60611

During the middle and late thirties, traditional Western production was drastically and decisively influenced by two interesting, perhaps slightly lunatic novelties. The first was the Gene Autry singing Westerns, and the second the remake of **Destry Rides Again** (Universal, 1939). The Autry films for Republic embodied what I have chosen to call the Autry-Fantasy, a world-view in which a dandified troubador in fancy semi-Western dress strums his way nonchalantly through veritable forests of villains, felling them with a song, outwitting them, but seldom shooting them. Autry, as a Western hero, was a mockery, subtle and intense, of everything that had gone before. His extreme popularity wasn't due so much to the fact that he sang, as to the vivid fairy-tale content of his films.

Destry Rides Again (Universal, 1939) advanced this notion of a mild-mannered hero who, by speaking softly and using his head, systematically exasperates and then defeats the far more powerful dens of heavies. Tom Mix had starred in the original film; he was dangerous and settled his scores by physical prowess. James Stewart, as Tom Destry, Jr., appears to be a laughing-stock and an incorrigible buffoon. But at the end of the film, he has reduced chief villain Brian Donlevy and his evil horde to total capitulation through a raid on the saloon by the ladies' aid society. Marlene Dietrich was cast as a dance hall queen and sang a few songs. Her career was in eclipse, but **Destry Rides Again** restored her to favor for the next decade.

Because of the astonishing success of the humorous, musical satire in **Destry**, Universal thought they could follow it with another winner stamped from the same mold, only furthering the comic ingredients. The result was **My Little Chickadee**.

The critical response to **Chickadee** has varied over the years. Robert Lewis Taylor in his book on W. C. Fields says the film was "mostly made . . . up as they went along. There was a good deal of professional antagonism between the two authors." William K. Everson in his book *The Art of W. C. Fields* comments, "As was usual with both of them, Mae West and Fields insisted on writing their own stories, and the collaboration proved to be a smooth one."

It is a constant cause of wonder to me where most writers on the cinema get their information. There are two quite valuable sources in the present instance, Mae West's comments in her revised autobiography and Universal Pictures' legal file on the film. In addition to all of the copyright and contractual information, the file also contains the original shooting script and the cutting continuities based on the contents of the actual release print.

Every Day's a Holiday was Mae's last major picture. Her terms to renew her contract with Cohen had been the making of a color production based on her story idea, *Catherine Was Great*. Cohen would hear nothing of it. She was released. An independent corporation was set up whose objective would be the projected picture's manufacture, but the film was never made. It might have been an unconditional box-office smash in 1933, but by 1940 the Hays Office had thoroughly thwarted Mae's motion picture career.

"You're still the hottest thing in town," Jim Timony assured her.

But even Timony realized, as Mae did, that her material was in need of a vital alteration, a fresh perspective. What was popular about Mae's early Paramount films wasn't their Gay Nineties settings, but Mae's satirical commentary on life. She tried to update herself to a contemporary background with *Go West, Young Man*, but it was only a partial success. Hers was a comedy based on exploding inhibitions and hypocrisies. Her brilliant repartee distinguished her from all hip-swinging imitators. The Hays Office was in effect forcing her back to the legitimate stage, but in 1940 neither she nor her manager acknowledged it.

Universal Pictures approached her with a proposal to make a picture with W. C. Fields. She accepted the offer, but had certain provisions incorporated into her starring contract. There was to be no drinking on the set by Fields, and he was to be barred if he even smelled of liquor. Mae was to have story approval and was empowered to make dialogue changes, but at no additional cost to the studio. She was given first position on the credits.

Mr. Fields's cinematic career is one of the most unusual of any Hollywood comedian. He developed a wholly consistent, if somewhat jaundiced, view of life which he set forth in films that have made more money since his death than upon initial release. I may be censured for saying so, but the film was, it seems to me, uniquely his medium. Within its scope, he combined the acute, scathing realism that Maugham most readily achieved in his short stories, the preposterous chicanery of Falstaff without Shakespeare's poetry, the outspoken, caustic wit of Dorothy Parker's essays, and the hilarious satire of social convention true of Aldous Huxley's early novels. In a personal sense, Fields's soul was deeply troubled by his knowledge of men, and the cruelty of his comedy was as nothing compared to his cruelty toward practically everyone around him. John Barrymore lamented, on his last trip to the hospital, that he would never see Uncle Willie again, but he was one of the few. W. C. Fields drank himself to death, and there are those today who have a good laugh at his expense, just as Fields parodied in his last films the shambles to which years of alcoholism had reduced him. Mae in a moment of sentiment remarked, "I think that under the grotesque ruin of a clown Bill Fields was tragically aware of the wreck he had made of himself." Most people in the industry who knew Fields at all well didn't think that the spectacle of his life was especially funny.

When a man decides he doesn't want to live any longer, there sometimes is a twilight state before that decision resolves into a desire to die. Fields was in that state of mind during the filming of *Chickadee*. Mae West didn't particularly relish working with him, but I suspect her objection to Fields's alcoholism only veiled her deeper discomfort at his despair, his pitiable fear that she might steal a scene from him, the fragility with which he faced every situation that might rob him of a laugh. Everson, in his book, paints a portrait of Fields as a masterful performer, rather than the crushed, desperately amusing, disconsolate jester he really was, oppressed at every turn by an overwhelming dislike for people, for life, for consciousness itself, all of which was a source of perpetual anguish to him. His comedy is that of laughing amid the rubble of physical defeat; the amusement he engenders has about it a quality both lusty and hopeless.

How anyone could seriously entertain the notion of a film incorporating these two widely divergent personalities is puzzling. The stock Diamond Lil character could not integrate with Fields's screen image of the lovable, drunken rogue, so Mae, in writing the screenplay *The Lady and the Bandit* did a surprising thing. Both she and Willie objected violently to Universal's story-line in *The Jayhawkers*, which had originally inspired their joint casting. Mae had previously written plays in which she did not star. In *Chickadee,* which title she adopted to satisfy Field's desire for some mark of identity, she wrote what must be termed principally a Fields vehicle. It was also an experiment for Mae to see how far she could censor her comedy and devise a new screen characterization. In this she was not so effective as

in giving Fields an opportunity to create one of his most delightful performances.

Although they were both given screen credit for the story, Fields' new scenes came to little over four pages of dialogue. They were extraneous to the plot, like a similar sequence of Mae in a school-room which she wrote as a compensating solo presentation; Fields' material was shot after Mae's part in the production was over. Of his additions, Mae has written, "They were simply exaggerated tales of his bouts with booze. He also rephrased some of the speeches I had written for him. Altogether, it was estimated that his contribution to the script amounted to ten per cent of the 153-page screenplay." Fields was paid $25,000 for this extra material and $125,000 for his appearance. Mae was paid a flat $300,000 with an option to make the two remaining films on Fields's contract with Universal on a similar basis. The thinking here reflected Universal's overall concept of uniting box-office in a single production as they did in the Johnny Mack Brown Westerns which costarred Tex Ritter or the horror combinations like *House of Frankenstein* with five monsters for the price of one. Mae was dissatisfied and turned down the option. Yet, while *Chickadee* isn't a particularly good film for her, nor

is it especially funny, it has probably been seen by more of the present generation than any of her other films.

It was shot on the Universal lot, using their Western town set. The production cut corners wherever possible because of the increased size of stars' salaries. Mae had the first reel to herself; in the rest Fields more or less predominated. He was removed from the set but once due to drunkenness. He was discovered hanging around the stage door encouraging young children to play in the street in front of moving cars. His attitude toward Mae was at first comradely, then awed, then indifferent, and it shows up in the film. Fields may have got most of the laughs, but, whereas he frequently outwits the other players, Flower Belle consistently makes a fool of him. Even in the demoralized state of his private life, Fields, although apparently keeping his own counsel, was wounded by his loss of dignity. Miss West reacted adversely to Fields's invariably boozy exuberance. One of the reasons her scenes with him don't always come off is the temperamental disdain she inwardly felt toward him. On the set she remarked, "Bill's a good guy, but it's a shame he has to be so goddamned cute." Years later she responded to the suggestion that she

had made more than one film with Fields, "No way, baby. Once was enough."

Mae's plot, before actual production, emphasized her romance with the masked bandit; during shooting this aspect became secondary. I will give no more than a brief outline of the story, not only because it is familiar to most, but also because it has been recounted in detail in the books about Fields.

Flower Belle is abducted from a stagecoach by a masked bandit, played by Joseph Calleia. When she is returned, her attitude is one of such obvious pleasure that before long she is asked to leave town. The local women's group telegraphs ahead to her intended destination of Greasewood City, warning the Ladies' Aid Society of her arrival. Everson remarks on the reminiscent quality of this sequence to that in *Stagecoach* (United Artists, 1939) in which Claire Trevor is similarly run out of town. More importantly, Mae was trying to make her persecution by the self-righteous ladies' groups humorous; if it could be reduced to a joke, its sting would be lessened.

Fields, being dragged on a stretcher by a donkey led by an Indian, blocks the track and boards the train. En route, the train is attacked by Indians. This footage is filmed in the finest tradition of the justly praised Universal action Westerns. Flower Belle takes up a pair of .45's and blazes away, felling countless marauding redskins. "There he goes in a shower of feathers," she comments, as another brave hits the ground.

Cuthbert J. Twillie, the character name Fields preferred to Mae's Nesselrode, is a travelling con man with a satchel apparently loaded with yellowbacks; the money turns out later to be coupons entitling the bearer to a discount on Fields's patent medicines. Flower Belle arranges a marriage ceremony for the two of them aboard the train, performed by Donald Meek, a card sharp. Not only will this give her access to Twillie's money, but a legitimacy that will permit her to enter Greasewood City unmolested.

At the hotel, the bride books two rooms. Flower Belle locks Twillie out of her boudoir. "Egad," Twillie remarks, "the child's afraid of me . . . she's all a'twit." He bends down to peer through the keyhole. "I have certain very definite pear-shaped ideas to discuss with you," he announces. Flower Belle opens the door with such abruptness that Twillie does a pratfall. She makes it clear that his moment of bliss must be postponed. Disappointed, Twillie heads for the saloon, passing

his stoical Indian companion on the way. "New squaw?" the Indian asks. "New is right," Twillie responds. "She hasn't even been unwrapped yet."

Calleia is the saloon owner. Flower Belle enters and they become fast friends. She persuades Calleia to save Twillie from reprisals come of card cheating. Twillie is made sheriff.

Fuzzy Knight, a Universal contract player of comic roles in their Western series, shows up and tells Twillie he is Flower Belle's cousin Zeb. Twillie talks him into a card game. "Is this a game of chance?" Fuzzy asks. "Not the way I play it," Twillie returns, "no-o."

At a banquet thrown for the new sheriff in which Twillie is assigned a place in a closet, Flower Belle sings her song "Willie of the Valley" and carries on her affair with Calleia. That night Flower Belle appears to soften toward Twillie. In her room at last, Twillie decides to take a bath in preparation for the joyous moment. While he is telling his usual tall tales and soaking, Flower Belle hides a goat in the marriage bed and slips off to see her lover. "Keep your mouth closed," she tells the goat, "and let him do all the talking . . . Do this right and I'll get you his straw hat."

A fantastically funny episode ensues, as Twillie attempts to make love to the goat. Presently, the goat having grown bored and bolted, Twillie's restless slumbers are interrupted by some of the townsfolk pounding on his door. He agrees to raise a posse, but goes back to bed. "Sleep," he says, "the most beautiful experience in life—except drink."

At this point, Fields's bartending skit is injected. The persistent stories about Flower Belle's romance with the masked bandit lead Twillie to disguise himself in just such an outfit and clamor noisily up a ladder to Flower Belle's room. He is met with ardent embraces and kisses. But the kind of kisses he gives and his protruberant, red proboscis expose him. Flower Belle denounces his calumny. "Anything worth having is worth cheating for," he replies.

Twillie is observed in his bandit costume and the town vigilantes promptly arrest him. "I was at a masquerade party," he pleads, "impersonating a Ubangi." He is sentenced to hang. The noose is placed around his neck. "This will be a great lesson to me," he comments in response to a question concerning his last sentiments. "Cuthbert J. Twillie for sheriff!" he says. Asked if he has any final request, he retorts, "Yes, I'd like to see Paris before I die." The noose tightens. "Philadelphia will do."

Above: With Joseph Calleia as the Masked Bandit

Between Margaret Hamilton and Dick Foran

With Dick Foran and Joseph Calleia

Flower Belle in the meantime convinces the real masked bandit to make an appearance, thus exonerating Twillie. Calleia goes farther. He not only appears; he even returns the stolen loot. Twillie is released. Mae had a good sense of theatre. Her gesture here makes up for any abusive treatment she may have submitted Twillie to earlier.

Dick Foran, a Universal Western star, plays Wayne Carter, an honest newspaper man. He wants to get the goods on Calleia. He also has a crush on Flower Belle. He vies with Calleia for her attentions. At the end of the film, Flower Belle reveals to Twillie the fraud of their marriage. She is passionately courted by her two suitors. Twillie decides to go back East with a new scheme, selling shares in hair-oil wells. Twillie tells Flower Belle to "C'mon up and see me sometime." She promises she will, calling him "my little chickadee." This gag closes on Mae's swaying bottom as she mounts the stairs, "The End" appearing across it, harking back to her entrance into films in *Night After Night*.

Mae was very much a box-office asset to the picture. It outgrossed most of Fields's Universal comedies, although *The Bank Dick* is a better entry for him. There is something strange about *Chickadee*. The dialogue and the situations constantly promise to provide more comedy than they do. As placid as their relations are on screen, I suspect that the fault in *Chickadee* lies in the antipathy between Bill Fields and Mae in terms of temperament and personality. They are essentially unfunny as a team, however good each is at comedy alone. There is no magic interplay, and so there is less than everyone had a right to anticipate.

The men in the casting department, conscious of what clear, strong types both performers projected on screen, thought teaming them incredibly funny. But once the initial joke is over, Mae and Willie, if they are funny at all, are funny separately, or just not funny. It was on the basis of this experience, I believe, that Mae satisfied herself that she couldn't come to rely on a screen characterization about whom amusing things are said, but who usually does not say them; or comic situations amusing in themselves, but not because of the presence of the articulate comedy at which she was uncommonly adept.

The Heat's On

Columbia, 1943
Running time: 80 minutes.

Producing company Columbia Pictures
Producer **Gregory Ratoff**
Associate Producer Milton Carter
Director **Gregory Ratoff**
Assistant director Robert Sanders
Dialogue director Serge Bertensson
Original story Boris Ingster, Lou Breslow
Screenplay Fitzroy Davis, George S. George, Fred Schiller
Musical director Yasha Bunchuk
Songs and lyrics Jay Gorney, Edward Eliscu, Jule Styne, Sammy Cahn
Original Music John Leipold
Art director Lionel Banks, Walter Holscher
Production designer Nicolai Remisoff
Set decoration Joseph Kish
Costumes Walter Plunkett
Choreography David Lichine
Film editor Otto Meyer
Sound engineer Lodge Cunningham

CAST

Fay Lawrence Mae West
Hubert Bainbridge Victor Moore
Tony Ferris William Gaxton
Xavier Cugat Himself
Hazel Scott Herself
Mouse Beller Lester Allen
Forrest Stanton Allan Dinehart
Janey Bainbridge (Jane Adair) Mary Roche
Andy Walker Lloyd Bridges
Hannah Bainbridge Almira Sessions
Frank Sam Ash
Extras Leonard Sues, Jack Owen, Joan
    Thorsen, Lina Romay, Roy Engel,
    Harry O. Tyler, Harry Shannon,
    Leon Balasco, Edward Earle, Harry
    Harvey

Current owner world rights: Columbia Pictures Corporation

(Note: Prints of this film are not presently available nontheatrically. It is obtainable to television through Screen Gems, the television subsidiary of Columbia Pictures. While retaining all rights, the negative to this film has been donated to the United States of America for deposit at the Library of Congress by Columbia Pictures Corporation. The film entered production in October 1943, and was put into release on 9 February 1944.)

One day in early 1943, Gregory Ratoff, who had played Pinkowitz in *I'm No Angel* and was by then a producer and director, showed up at Mae's apartment with her agent; he had an offer for a new picture. Mae hadn't been on the screen since *My Little Chickadee*. Ratoff had a lot of enthusiasm which carried him over the fact that he had an unclear story idea. The name of the picture was to be *Tropicana*, and it was ostensibly to be based on a successful Broadway show. Mae agreed conditionally, provided the plot-line proved acceptable. Due to the fact that Ratoff was busy with a film for MGM release, Mae waited weeks for the delivery of the script.

Ratoff returned in person, filled with apologies for the delay and excuses about the story. " 'Dollink,' " Mae quotes him as saying in her autobiography, " 'we can't make the story I told you, but the name *Tropicana* we'll make.' " He told her a new story he had in mind and made it sound good enough for Mae to sign a contract without seeing any more than him.

Production began at once at Columbia with the shooting of the musical numbers. Ratoff managed, despite his hurry, to fire off a copy of the completed screenplay to Mae. Publicity was already being issued concerning a new Mae West picture. Mae herself was interviewed by the press. "You can do a good thing just so many times," she confided, "before people begin to ask themselves: 'Where have I seen that before?' Well, that's the way I felt about my Diamond Lil characterization. I played the same role in nine pictures. I gave the role every different shading and meaning I could. I honestly think I have exhausted all its possibilities. . . . You know, it's a funny thing. When I first came to Hollywood, and wanted to do *She Done Him Wrong*, they told me fans would never go for that period stuff. The modern generation wanted something zippy and new. The success of the formula proved I was right. Diamond Lil went over with a bang. And now I'm just as convinced I shouldn't repeat a tenth time."

But when Mae read Ratoff's scenario, she was furious. The story conceived of her role in a very unfavorable light and, if done, would be ruinous to the popular image she had created throughout her career. She asked to be released from her contract. Ratoff reasoned with her. He had expended considerable funds on just the musical numbers and now was prepared to shoot the main scenes with the principals. The bank backing of the production would not permit him to change the star when it had financed the venture only because the film was a Mae West vehicle. According to Mae, Ratoff pleaded in three languages.

The most ominous factor was Ratoff's threatened bankruptcy if Mae refused to go through with the picture. Mae neither wanted to be blamed for his unfortunate circumstances nor for it to be thought in Hollywood that she had become intemperate and unreliable. The consideration became which would hurt her reputation more, Ratoff's incipient ruin, or a bad picture? She agreed to do the picture if she was allowed to rewrite all of her scenes. Ratoff foolishly consented, foolishly because he had shot extensively from a screenplay that would now be radically revised, because he was going to end up with two pictures in one, and it has never worked out when a star writes his or her part in contrast to the screenplay's conception of how that part integrates with the whole. Such a production would die at the box office even if Mae was in it. Ratoff should have known Mae well enough to have guessed that she would want to handle her own part, and attempted to build his picture around her, if he wanted her in it. If he didn't, the truth is that a dozen or more musicals had been made on precisely the theme he was employing in his screenplay and he could have blithely made the thirteenth. Instead, he insisted on putting a special kind of talent into an unspecial kind of picture, which could do neither the talent nor the picture any good. Lastly, because of his manipulations, Ratoff was too strapped for money to start over, which he would have had to do in order to assure a box office success. *The Heat's On*, when it finally emerged, was stillborn, revealing painfully the contradictory genesis it had had, memorable perhaps for no other reason. Mae wrote a few dazzling scenes, but out of eighty minutes was on camera exactly twenty-four minutes and forty-two seconds, not enough to make it a Mae West picture. The story dragged.

Here is Ratoff's original story before Mae went to work on it. *Indiscretions*, a Broadway play, is a flop. Despite Tony Ferris producing and Fay Lawrence starring, unlike their previous five hits, the show is a lemon. Sid Martin, Tony's financial backer, wants to close. Fay, too, wants out. Tony is guzzling Bromo-Seltzer in his office when Hubert Bainbridge comes to see him. The Bainbridge Foundation exists as a private organization to police public morals, run by Hubert's sister, Hannah. Hubert is her kid brother, although middle-aged, and supervises the supply room.

Tony thinks Hubert wants to complain about *Indiscretions*. Far from it! Hubert likes the show. He wants to ask Ferris a favor. Will Ferris help promote Hubert's young niece into show business? She is a natural talent, supposedly, but smothered by her job at the Foundation. Tony is about to throw Hubert out when an idea occurs to him. Why not stage a police raid, at the insistence of the Foundation? The publicity might be exactly the thing the show needs.

Hubert agrees and the next night *Indiscretions* is raided. The police take Fay off to jail. She suspects a rat when Tony escapes. He promises to get her out at once, but doesn't. Instead he leaves her to spend the night in the clink. By morning the newspapers are carrying the headline that Fay Lawrence is a martyr. When Tony stops at the jail to see her, he explains his action as a promotional stunt. Fay is irked and doesn't believe him. The crowds swarm the box office but it is to no avail when the police serve notice that the city has undertaken a morals campaign in view of the attitude of the Bainbridge Foundation and *Indiscretions* is one of four shows being permanently closed.

Tony is back in his office, consuming Bromos, when Hubert appears with little Janey Bainbridge for her audition. He is rather proud of the raid and shocked to find that Tony isn't happy with the results. Tony gives them the brush-off. In the meantime, the papers announce that a second-rate producer named Stanton has signed Fay Lawrence to appear in a new musical called *Tropicana*. Tony goes wild with rage. He and his sidekick Mouse dream up a scheme to lure Fay back. Tony climbs into bed at his apartment and pretends he is dying from an overdose of sleeping pills. Mouse brings Fay to see him. However Tony's enthusiasm about producing another show makes Fay suspicious as to the seriousness of his condition and when, in his joy at her verbal agreement, Tony jumps out of bed fully clothed, Fay turns her back on him and leaves.

Tony goes to Hubert, who is acting vice president of the Foundation while his sister is out of town, and promises Janey the lead in *Tropicana* if Hubert will cooperate. Hubert concurs and at Tony's instigation phones Stanton to inform him that Fay Lawrence is on the Foundation's blacklist. Stanton willingly sells Tony his show for $10,000. But Fay, learning of the change in producers, will not honor her contract, and quits. Tony gets Hubert to back the show with Foundation funds, now starring Janey under the

With Beatrice Blinn and Victor Moore

With Victor Moore

With Almira Sessions and Victor Moore

name Jane Adair. All indications are that Jane will be a smash hit.

Fay is angered by this new course of events. She has a case of Bromo-Seltzer sent to Tony, ostensibly from the manufacturer, and then notifies him that rat poison was delivered instead. Tony believes he's dying and in his agony is persuaded by Fay to sign his show over to Sid Martin. No sooner does she get his signature, than a representative of Bromo-Seltzer appears and sets the record straight. It's too late for Tony, though, because Fay has his contract and *Tropicana* is scheduled to open with Fay in the lead. Jane Adair is through before she gets her chance. Tony plays his final card on opening night. Jane's soldier boyfriend has filled up two-thirds of the theatre with his military buddies. Unless Fay steps aside, and lets Jane have her chance, they'll boo her off the stage. Fay gives in. Jane does the show successfully, and the story ends with Fay reassuming the lead of *Tropicana* for a successful run.

There was no way Mae could have responded positively to an unsympathetic role like that of Fay Lawrence. It suggested she was guileful, a has-been, selfish, and capable of being outwitted not by one man but by several. Had Ratoff and his writers, Boris Ingster and Lou Breslow, deliberately sought to concoct a scenario destructive to the Mae West format, they couldn't have done better.

So now Ratoff had his musical numbers, and it was up to Mae to rewrite Fay Lawrence's scenes so as to preserve what she wanted. As difficult as it is to compose a sonnet, to get a story to encompass all the musical numbers and expensive footage Ratoff had filmed, and yet alter the meaning of everything, takes more ingenuity. Mae did her best, but ultimately it couldn't save the picture. Here is the story as it was finally released.

The viewer is brought right into the middle of a song and dance number from *Indiscretions*. The show is a flop according to everyone's comments. Tony visits Fay after the performance and she tells him that she has a tradition of success to live up to and his show isn't helping her do it. Tony then goes to his office and meets with Hubert, and they plot the raid. Hubert persuades his sister to act, but Fay isn't at the theatre when the raid occurs. The next morning she pulls up in her chauffeured car and Tony comes out to assure her that the raid was only a publicity gimmick. When the ban becomes permanent, there's a cut to the Casa Cugat and a musical number. Cugat tells Tony and Mouse that he has been signed for the new Forrest Stanton production, *Tropicana*, starring Fay Lawrence.

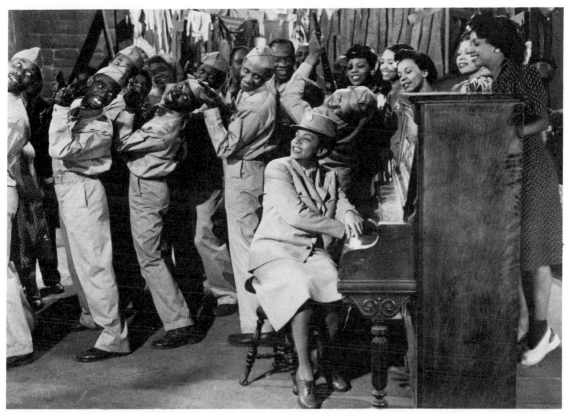
Hazel Scott at the piano

Tony decides to peek at the new show during rehearsal. Cut to a Jane Adair number that doesn't really make sense. Tony is worried and so drops by the Foundation, where Hubert is acting in his sister's absence as an overseer. Tony has him phone Stanton and tell him that Fay is blacklisted. Cut to the Casa Cugat and another number, after which Stanton sells Tony the show for $10,000. Tony quiets Hubert's conscience and gets the Foundation's backing by promising Janey a role. Cut now to rehearsals, number after musical number. Hazel Scott is in two of them.

Fay meets Hubert at the stage door, invites him to her apartment, and, getting him to confess that his family made its money in hair tonic, he finally tells her the plot. Fay tips off Stanton who calls Hubert's sister in Washington. Cut to another long series of production numbers, including one with Hubert and Janey called "A Little Bit of Corn." Hannah storms into the theatre and pulls both Janey and Hubert out with her. Tony is left destitute, no money, no show, no Jane Adair, and no Fay Lawrence. With Mouse's assistance, Tony dreams up an idea to get Fay back. He pretends that he had a nervous breakdown and Mouse brings Fay to the sanitarium to see him. Fay isn't fooled. She agrees to star in *Tropicana* but tells the psychiatrist to keep Tony locked up, which he is only too happy to do.

Fay visits Hannah at the Foundation and gets her to back the show, observing, "You're holding the bag. You may as well have something in it." There is some amusing dialogue.

> *Hannah:* My ancestors came over on the *Mayflower.*
> *Fay:* You're lucky. Now they have immigration laws.

When at last Fay threatens to expose Hubert's role in the whole thing publicly, Hannah gives in. Fay advises Janey that anyone can have a career, despite her aunt's opposition or that of her boyfriend. Cut to the grand production number with which the picture ends, the finale to an immensely successful *Tropicana.*

Was Mae West right in making the picture, even with her emendations? The plot had no substance and less interest; the musical numbers were unintegrated and retarded what little story-line there was. Mae wrote in her autobiography, "After this dismal experience I made up my mind that I would never do another picture unless everything, but everything, was to my satisfaction, and so stipulated in black and white, without an accent." It was fully twenty-seven years before she made another film, and, as in the case of *The Heat's On*, it did not prove to be totally to her liking.

"Hello Mi Amigo"

Myra Breckinridge

20th Century-Fox, 1970
Running time: 95 minutes

Producing company   20th Century-Fox
Producer   Robert Fryer
Director   Michael Sarne
From the novel by   Gore Vidal
Screenplay   Michael Sarne, David Giler
Music supervised and conducted   Lionel Newman
Song: "Secret Place"
Lyrics and music   John Phillips
Photography   Richard Moore
Choreography   Ralph Beaumont
Costumes   Theadora Van Runkle
Miss West's costumes   Edith Head
Art directors   Jack Martin Smith, Fred Harpman
Set decorators   Walter M. Scott, Reg Allen
Makeup supervision   Dan Striepeke
Makeup artist   Del Acevedo
Hair stylist   Edith Lindon
Orchestration   Jack Elliott, Jeff Alexander, Allyn Ferguson, Lyn Murray
Film editor   Danford B. Greene
Unit production manager   William Eckhardt
Assistant director   Dick Glassman
Sound   Don Bassman, Dave Dockendorf
Special photographic effects   L.B. Abbott, A.S.C.; Art Cruickshank, A.S.C.
Unit publicist   Don Prince
Filmed in   Panavision
Color by   DeLuxe
Titles by   Pacific Title

CAST

Letitia Van Allen   Mae West
Buck Loner   John Huston
Myra   Raquel Welch
Young Man (Myron)   Rex Reed
Mary-Ann   Farrah Fawcett
Dr. Montag   Roger C. Carmel
Rusty   Roger Herren
Charlie Flager, Jr.   George Furth
Irving Amadeus   Calvin Lockhart
Doctor   Jim Backus
Surgeon   John Carradine
Coyote Bill   Andy Devine
Kid Barlow   Grady Sutton
Charlie Flager, Sr.   Robert Lieb
Chance   Skip Ward
Bobbie Dean Loner   Kathleen Freeman
Tex   B.S. Pully
Jeff   Buck Kartalian
Vince   Monty Landis
Mae's secretary   Tom Selleck
Student   Peter Ireland
Mario   Nelson Sardelli
Judge   William Hopper
Cameo in dentist's chair   Genevieve ("Joanna") Waite
Cameo in posture class   Michael Sarne

(Note: Released in July 1970, the film had a negative cost of $5,500,000, and is still in release worldwide. Oddly enough, credits were not supplied for the many clips and sound track rerecordings used in the release print. This practice has so generally resulted in an infinitude of law suits from parties who have felt their image being misused that Fox escaped lightly with trouble only from Shirley Temple and Loretta Young. Billing footage, given in the text, ran originally to 8,930 ft. of 35mm. stock, while picture-to-picture was a flat 8,500 ft. Production began on 23 September 1969 and concluded on 26 February 1970. Mae's songs were shot on 19 March 1970.)

Current owner world rights: 20th Century-Fox Film Corporation.
Prints of this film are available from: FILMS, INCORPORATED, 1144 WILMETTE AVENUE, WILMETTE, ILLINOIS 60091, ATTN: ALLEN GREEN.

Myra Breckinridge might have been a great film. Instead it was doomed to be a box-office bomb. Some of the sequences which survived the cutting room are engaging cinema. But it had too much against it, from the start. While purporting to be a story about the total realization of *phantasy,* as the psychologists call it, the picture is painfully realistic in a way that could never hope to be popular. Moviegoers have always demanded *fantasy,* as the storytellers prefer it, from the motion picture. Reality is acceptable to a mass audience provided it is outshown at every turn by fantasy, or, at the very least, done in at the end with fantasy ultimately triumphant.

I cannot but be somewhat sympathetic with popular expectations. After all, if an artist insists on showing reality in unadorned nakedness, his "showing" should be sufficiently pleasant to attract enough people willing to pay for the experience to support his creation. Too many young filmmakers seem to be childishly hostile to their prospective audiences. Michael Sarne's major directorial credit before *Myra* was *Joanna*, produced by Laughlin Films, Ltd., and distributed in the United States through the Fox exchanges. About a fashion model, it was like a long string of pilots for television commercials, full of burner-out frames, slow-motion photography, and a black and white pseudo-orgy scene. Fox publicity built the picture up as exactly what the "now" generation was looking for in a film, and then it died at the dollar sign. Fox was perhaps more guilty of believing their publicity about Sarne's appeal for the youth market than anyone else.

Myra Breckinridge cost over $5,000,000 and told viewers something they obviously would rather not know and, under Michael Sarne's zealous screenplay and direction, told it in a way bound to be offensive. Offensive to what? to whom? To propriety, the Establishment, residual religious conservatism, prudery, middle-class morality? None of these. Gore Vidal's novel sold more than five and a half million copies. It was a book supposedly intended for the "now" generation. If as many people went to see the film as read the book, the picture would more than break even.

Vidal was paid $400,000 for the screen rights. Sarne's interpretation and direction have about them a literal faithfulness to *his* notion of the text that matches Von Stroheim's adherence to *McTeague* in filming **Greed**. But the edited version which was finally released altered the emphasis substantially. The lunacies of the "now" generation became the subject of ridicule, far more than the inadequacies of the generations of the recent past. The "now" generation has as much sense of humor as one of Hawthorne's dour Puritans; if anything, the audiences composed of "modern" hipsters, middle-aged women in miniskirts and mod hairdos, and middle-aged men in razor cuts and "jungle" clothes felt themselves being laughed at. The "now" generation takes itself very seriously, as Myra does the fact that she "is a real dish, and don't you forget it, all you mother-*bleep*-as the children say nowadays." Only the few who can laugh at *all* social artifices could join into the spirit of the film. There simply weren't enough of them to rack up impressive grosses. Sex films were doing business, and the more sex the better. *Myra Breckinridge*'s failure proved that sex film-goers weren't ready for a parody of sex, much less a satire on their own special mores.

Citizen Kane, like *Myra Breckinridge*, is an antisocial picture that, also like it, bombed at the box office. For all I know, the alienated critics and academics of a future time may declare *Myra* a screen classic for its truthfulness, as they now do *Kane*. It has one basic thing going for it. It didn't make money, which means it can be properly understood only by a select few. To this group truth must be ugly, or at least unpleasant, a gleeful condemnation, an exposure of imagined hypocrisy. This kind of truth assuages their bruised, ineffectual, adolescent egos. As if to prove this trend, *Myra* is doing good business nontheatrically on college campuses.

Mae West got top billing for *Myra*, although her part in the release print is anything but significant. She also rewrote her role to suit herself. Of the many confusions in the manufacture of the film, this one produced the most interesting consequences. Mae's alterations changed Letitia's essential character, thereby upsetting the vital balance her interplay established in the novel in terms of her role in plot progression. In view of Sarne's literalism in every other aspect of the production, the result is that we have a Mae West picture within a totally different kind of film. But her part is encompassed by the rest of the picture, just as are the clips from vintage features thrown in to make up for the scenes Fox executives scrapped. So we are left with a Mae West vehicle, a medley of old picture favorites, and a disconnected story of seduction in a phony acting academy, all spliced together.

In the pressbook released by Fox publicity,

there is an interview with Mae. "I have always campaigned for equal bedroom rights for women. The whole Mae West thing is founded on this. Women should be allowed sexual selection and sexual freedom!" She goes on. "In *Myra Breckinridge*, I meet a passionate young student who, in Gore Vidal's book, puts me in the hospital. In the version I have written I put *him* in the hospital! See what I mean?"

I do not know how Mae could have done otherwise with Letitia's part and still remained Mae West. Her rewritten role certainly reversed Michael Sarne's reading of Vidal's novel, but was perhaps more consistent with the spirit of the book. Sarne wanted to shoot the story as he interpreted it. With Mae in the cast, he couldn't; nor could Mae let him shoot her part as he proposed and still get her idea across. The upshot was strife during production, the picture running way over schedule. Sarne, angered by what he deemed Mae's interference, tried editing her out of the picture when he had spent $3,000,000 over his $2,500,000 budget, but lost out to financial considerations—as well he might. Richard Zanuck realized that the box-office value of *Myra Breckinridge* was Mae West, not Michael Sarne. Motion picture directors who are *auteurs* are so in film critics' minds, seldom on somebody else's five million dollars.

The problem was an insoluble one. Mae West and Michael Sarne were working from different perspectives. Had Mae's perspective dominated, I believe the picture would have enjoyed a successful run. Had Mae not been in it and Sarne shot it as a straight sex exploitation film, it might have done business with the male-oriented sex market. But the way he did shoot it, with the plot reaching its highpoint at the sexual congress between two males, it had the effect of turning *that* audience off.

Robert Fryer put two female sex symbols into an essentially homosexual drama, hoping, no doubt, that heterosexual audiences would be attracted (presumably this group is still in the majority). But once attracted, the film depicts the wooing and seduction of one male by another male. After Raquel Welch "deflowers" Rusty, Letitia in turn sexually exhausts him. In short, Rusty is reduced to a state of sexual prostration. When Mae was originally approached with the film, thinking it might be the lead, she said, "I like my sexes stable." But that's just what went wrong with the picture. Sex became wholly unstable. The sexual object in the film becomes Rusty for men and women alike, and he simply isn't up to it.

Michael Sarne's concept of *Myra Breckinridge* comes out in the way he finally put all of the pieces of the film together. The plot is very simple. Myron (Rex Reed), a homosexual film critic, undergoes an operation to become a woman. He goes to his Uncle Buck Loner's academy and tries to shake him down. Loner resists, and the ante keeps rising. Finally, showing his artificially manufactured vagina, he wins the money. In the interim, he seduces Rusty, and falls in love with Rusty's girl friend Mary-Ann. The sequences of Myra first coming to Buck's academy, or her scenes with Loner, or the seduction of Rusty are almost exactly as written in the novel. But in putting them together with the old film clips, with other scenes not in the book, and with scenes, such as the orgy, that may have been shot according to the text but now are severely edited, the satire and meaning of the novel are transformed. Robert Fryer is quoted as telling a reporter, "Michael Sarne . . . talks a good game, but he didn't know what he was doing. What I visualized when I read the book did not appear on the screen."

I think this was the general impression of everyone who had both read the book and seen the movie. Not that motion pictures need follow the original source slavishly. But if there was any message in *Myra Breckinridge*, or a meaning, or even a coherent story, it didn't end up in the release print. Rex Reed murmurs "Secret Place" during castration, and then frequently appears simultaneously with Myra.

Vidal has Myra say in the book, "The new American woman . . . uses men the way they once used women." Mae's dialogue is in this spirit, but not Sarne's screenplay. There is only one suggestion that Myra is busy raping men. Mae sings two rock numbers, elaborately staged, shot at the very end of production. She uses an all-Negro chorus for the choreography. But they are never integrated into the film. The viewer, accepting her role as a talent agent, doesn't quite know why she's singing them, nor is any explanation ever supplied—another instance of the disjointed structure of the film.

Buck Loner is a former singing cowboy, a lecher, and the unscrupulous owner of an acting school where all the misfits pay their tuition and never graduate to anything beyond being students. In the book, Loner is Vidal's most brilliant creation, and the satire concerning him is especially hilarious. Not only is his "academy" a symbol for all higher education in this country, where students stay in school until at last they attain to being

With Rex Reed, Raquel Welch, Robert Fryer, John Huston and Michael Sarne

"I'll tell you this though: In ten years I won't put up with this kind of crap."

—MICHAEL SARNE
on completion of the tenth screenplay for MYRA BRECKINRIDGE.

"It could be just awful if it isn't funny."

—ROBERT FRYER
after viewing disappointing Sarne rushes.

teachers to other students, but like our colleges and universities, the curriculum at Buck's institution isn't a preparation for life at all, just a high-priced substitute for it. Students, for a fee, are protected from all the pains and torments of reality. They have their own closed-circuit television programs which they produce and perform for; their own newspapers for which they are interviewed; their own award system for "stunning" performances. At his best, Vidal in **Myra Breckinridge** approaches a

combination of Lewis Carroll, Jonathan Swift, and Aldous Huxley. He deserved his success with the book. His bitter commentary on phantasy is fanciful enough to be entertaining without ever compromising its integrity.

The screenplay, for one reason or another, has none of this fine Loner interplay. In the novel, Buck is married to his former costar Bobbie Dean, modeled on Dale Evans, even to Bible-thumping. Bobbie becomes a Jehovah's Witness after an

161

With John Huston

illuminating bout with lesbianism. Kathleen Freeman played Bobbie in the film, but she got cut out of everything save the credits. A few lines are accurately paraphrased from the novel, as when Myra tells Buck "and so I must conclude that what you have assembled here are the national dregs, the misfits, the neurotics, the daydreamers, the unrealists, the, in short, fuckups . . . [of] our culture." But the essence of Buck's rather earthy, conniving personality, seated atop a Palomino stuffed for exhibition, as Roy Rogers has stuffed Trigger, with Gene Autry records playing in the background, is as little what it could have been as the whole tone of the parody. Sarne cameos himself in Myra's posture class.

Some of Mae's dialogue survives. When she meets a tall Texan, he volunteers his height as six feet, seven inches, and Letitia offers to talk to him about his "seven inches." When she is first seen parading down the aisle outside her talent agency, prospective leading men lined up on either side, she says, "I'll be right with ya, boys. Get out your *résumés*."

Letitia is colossally oversexed, a mature woman who tries out all the young hopefuls on a gigantic bed in her private office. Deleted from the release print are her lines, "You gotta mob here today and I'm a little tired. One of those guys'll have to go." When a dumb stud comes in and says all he wants is her respect, she comments, "Watch it, you're gonna kill the deal." She tells Myra, "The guy's a terrific bang. I wouldn't say he's exactly a sex maniac, but he'll do until one comes along." In the orgy sequence, badly cut, Letitia remarks, watching all of the young bodies engaged in varieties of sexual congress, "Umm, guess this is what they mean by lettin' it all hang out." In the Vietnam hospital scene, completely cut, one veteran complains to her about how his arm screws off and another that his leg screws off. She says, "Well, come up and see me sometime and I'll show you how to screw your *heads* off." One bit of dialogue did get through. When Letitia tells Myra she's to get an award, Myra asks her if it's an Oscar. "No, a golden phallus," adding: "Someday we'll have our own stable of studs—a boy bank where credit is always good. Sort of a lay-a-day plan." Myra says, "God bless America." The male sex-film addict likes one long romp through mounds of naked female bodies, usually on their backs. Is it any wonder they weren't laughing? *Myra Breckinridge* was fundamentally intended to lampoon male-oriented sex. Mae's rewritten part does just that.

Mae West and Raquel Welch didn't get along well. The friction between them was a constant source of gossip. When Robert Fryer introduced them, Mae extended a queenly hand, saying with a demure smile:

"Pleased to meetcha, sweetie. . . ."

"I'm so glad to meet you. I've admired you for so long," Raquel responded. Mae might have been nettled by the "so long." She didn't show it.

What notoriety Raquel had at the time came from showing off her body, which she admitted in a Fox publicity interview. Mae, in her interview, excerpted in *Playboy* (Jan., 1971) to promote the film, said: "My advice for those gals who think they have to take their clothes off to be a star is, baby, once you've boned, what's left to create an illusion? Let 'em *wonder*. I never believed in givin' 'em too much of me. I let the other woman in *Myra* do that."

Despite the clash, the fact remains that Mae has nonetheless become a success by using her head more than her body. In *Myra*, Raquel occasionally does funny things, as when she clobbers Buck Loner on the jaw. Huston's timing throughout is excellent. Mae confines her parody of sex to dialogue and its delivery. If she is a sex symbol, it is in the sense that sex has served as her story material. Her theatrical experience has taught her the importance of the imagination and how to use it to good effect.

Mae did not consider the film a comeback, although she had been off the screen for twenty-seven years. She brought with her to the set all of the opulent extravagance of a bygone Hollywood era. She rode in her own Rolls-Royce through several scenes. On the lot, she had her dressing room completely redecorated and a luxurious trailer followed her from stage to location. She was constantly agleam with diamonds. She was paid $350,000 for her part. Sarne got $75,000. For him it was his first important studio picture, and maybe his last for a while. Mae's songs were entitled "Hard to Handle" and "You've Gotta Taste All the Fruit." Over the credits Shirley Temple via rerecorded sound track sang, "On the Good Ship Lollipop."

Shirley was featured in a sequence that was later cut. In the scene where Myron, naked, is having a masturbatory phantasy in which Myra is performing fellatio on him, a clip from *Heidi* was inserted as he reaches climax in which Shirley Temple, attempting to milk a goat, squirts herself in the face. The White House demanded this be removed after the San Francisco preview, believing the implication offensive to the United Nations representative's public image.

Loretta Young also objected to her image being used, one a clip of a love scene between her and Clark Gable. Both clips, amounting to twelve feet, two frames each, were removed from all release prints after Fox settled the matter out of court, effective 3 August 1970. The Marlene Dietrich footage was obtained from MCA-Universal, and in this case Fox was asked to simply post a $5,000 bond and indemnify Universal. Laurel and Hardy in clips from their Fox features of the forties were played up as homosexuals, which met with some objections from fans. The entire Glenn Miller performance of the song "Chatanooga Choo-Choo" was clipped from *Sun Valley Serenade*, along with a Carmen Miranda number.

All of this footage was to give the picture a pop art collage look after Fox cutters finished with Sarne's work print. Among the more regrettable losses was the scene between Buck and Letitia in Letitia's bedroom office. While one may lament the excision of innocuous sequences from Mae's *Klondike Annie*, *Myra* is even more butchered. There will never be any reclaiming of the scrapped footage. Prior to Loretta Young's lawsuit, the film was mounted on twelve reels at 8,930 ft. of 35mm. stock running ninety-five minutes. Of this, almost thirty minutes were stock footage inserts and longish beginning and ending credit crawls. Surprisingly, Fox was opposed to the "X" rating the film received.

Myra was advertised as a Mae West film, with Mae getting by contract 100% billing in the first position, John Huston 100% billing in the second, Raquel Welch 100% in third position. Mae's fans were disappointed at her limited part, and it was insufficient in itself to attract continuing crowds. Fox released *Myra* in key cities, but after the first few weeks grosses fell off, exhibitors suffering under ten to eighteen-week engagements. It was only another in a long series of unsuccessful films which finally brought about a realignment of Fox executives, Richard Zanuck leaving for Warner Bros., Darryl F. Zanuck becoming chairman emeritus.

Mae's reappearance on the screen caused a

"You Gotta Taste All the Fruit"

considerable furor and there were rumors that she might remake *She Done Him Wrong*. Her autobiography was reissued, with new chapters bringing it up to date, in an extraordinarily large printing. Twentieth Century-Fox Records issued her songs. Whether due to her having too little control over the production (although the producer certainly wasn't in a better position, as things turned out), or simply the compounded comedy of errors surrounding the production, in no way can this film be considered as showing Mae at her best. Perhaps even with the rewriting, the part fundamentally wasn't congenial to her special brand of erotic humor. Wherever she went for premieres, she was mobbed, indications that the Mae West charisma had not faded.

Mae West Wed Secretly in 1911, She Confesses

(Special to The News)

Los Angeles, July 7.—Mae West of the buxom curves and the "C'm up" eyes abandoned her long-cherished role of spinsterhood today and admitted a marriage in Milwaukee to Frank Wallace, vaudeville hoofer, twenty-six long years ago. But it wasn't to take him back. Quite the contrary.

In replying to Wallace's suit asking that the court compel the wealthy actress to recognize him as her lawful spouse, the beguiling Mae set forth that not once, ever, had they lived together as man and wife and that Wallace, in 1916, took to wife Miss Ray Blakesly without first honoring Mae with a divorce.

A court decree dissolved the second marriage in 1935, however, when, according to Mae, "that man" decided to cut in on Mae's accumulating wealth. Hollywood reeled under today's disclosure. The Westian spinsterhood a myth? And twenty-six years ago—that was in 1911, wasn't it? Yep, April 11, in fact.

For twenty-six years Mae West kept a secret. But yesterday she admitted she married Frank Wallace in 1911.

Too Young in 1911?

Since Wallace first popped out of obscurity in New York in 1935 to sue for recognition, the quipful Mae has from time to time released bon mots like these:

Frank Wallace

"I never married Frank Wallace or anybody else. I was a school girl in 1911, too young to marry."

"I don't know that man and I never was married to him. After all, I should know ..."

"Peculiar, that every time one of my pictures is released, he shows up again."

Attached to Wallace's complaint was a copy of the marriage license they obtained in that far-off day, giving Mae's age then as 18. The table cloths in all the better restaurants in Hollywood tonight were marked up with the simple sums of 18 and 26, all adding up to 44.

A courtship in Canarsie, Wallace's suit set forth, preceded the marriage in Milwaukee. And in 1914, he added, he stepped out of her way, at her request, to permit her to pursue her career alone. All he wants now is his rightful recognition and a division of community property which he figures runs "well in excess of $100,000."

Feared Effect on Career.

At about the time Mae should have been celebrating her silver wedding anniversary, Wallace wrote her:

"I say to you sincerely, Mae, that my love and affection for you has never diminished and through the past years I have proven this by living up to the agreement we made that neither of us mention our marriage. You know that this agreement was made because you felt that if the public knew you were married, it would hinder your career."

Mae was not to be found tonight.

"Don't ever make the same mistake twice—unless it pays."
— Mae West

The Later Theatrical Career

Mae West was busy with her Empire Pictures project at the beginning of 1939. She was still thinking of **Catherine Was Great** in terms of a Technicolor extravaganza. James Timony turned his mind to producing a non-West play. It was titled **Clean Beds** and had a dubious authorship. George S. George was the credit given. *The New York Times* suggested that this was a pseudonym for a Youacca G. Satovsky. Others were mentioned as possible authors. Mae helped out by polishing the script somewhat. It opened at the John Golden Theatre in New York on 25 May 1939 and closed after four performances on 27 May 1939. The *New York Herald Tribune* commented that "the World's Fair will hardly find **Clean Beds** a rival." The *World-Telegram* added that it "signified the death of the 1938-39 season."

CLEAN BEDS

A Drama in Three Acts by George S. George. Produced by James A. Timony under the Name Cled, Inc.

CAST

Murrey   Nat Burns
Lodger   Edwin James
Worth   Joseph Holland
Goldie   Sheila Trent
Kelcy   William Balfour
Mrs. Murrey   Fifi Louise Hall
Jack Letton   Pat Gleason
Donald Tabor   Alfred Alderdie
Charlie   James Welch
Officer Ryan   Tom Gorman
Ira Skyse   William Phinney
Joe   Raymond Maxwell
Blowsy Mag   Emma Hunting
Petroni   Anthony Raimond
Barbara   Helen Beverly
Daisy   Mara Brooke
Callahan   William Hunter
Mrs. Perkins   Leila Romer
Mary   Geraldine Cooke

The marriage license

With Jim Timony in court

The plot told of Murrey, who runs a flop house in a large Eastern city, and his wife, who manages a bawdy house on the side. An upstanding young man named Donald Tabor becomes a lodger at Murrey's flop house after a fight with Barbara, his wife. Murrey and two henchmen drug Tabor and try to sell Barbara on a white slavery apprenticeship with Mrs. Murrey. Donald overcomes the drug at the last minute and sends for the police. He and Barbara are reunited.

In the book *The Foremost Films of 1939*, Frank Vreeland included mention of Empire Pictures, incorporated at Sacramento, and listed its board of directors. They were Miss West, Louis Lurie, who supplied most of the $5,000,000 capitalization, Ralph Picus, and James Timony. Nothing came of the projected film. Mae appeared in *My Little Chickadee* in 1940. Then, after the catastrophe of *The Heat's On*, she decided to bring *Catherine Was Great* to the legitimate stage.

Between pictures, she weathered another personal crisis. In September 1941, Frank Wallace, still her husband, brought a separate maintenance suit against her for $1,000 in monthly alimony. When the case was dismissed in a San Bernardino court, Superior Judge Charles

L. Allison presiding, Wallace waited until July 1942 and brought a second suit. This one added to the $1,000 a month, $25,000 in attorneys' fees, $2,500 in court costs, and a community property settlement, estimating its value at $1,000,000. Mae sued for a divorce and was granted an interlocutory decree. She settled with Wallace for a substantial sum. Wallace could boast in the end that he had accomplished one significant thing in his time: he had successfully exploited his wife. Every time Mae was emotional, she lost money, so she taught herself not to be emotional. It's a state of self-control most never learn.

When Marlene Dietrich appeared in Paramount's *The Scarlet Empress*, Josef von Sternberg, the director, chose a surrealistic format. The picture dealt with Catherine's life until the time she seized the throne. Mae West's play was set in the period from Catherine II's coronation in 1762 until the Council declared her "the Great." Mae stressed Catherine's administrative genius; how she used diamonds and her physical attractions to build a strong Russia and a loyal army; how she captivated Pugacheff, the leader of a peasant revolt against the Tsarina; how she successfully planned the strategy against the Turks; and how she improved the lot of the serfs.

The play, produced by Mike Todd, opened for a tryout at the Forrest Theatre in Philadelphia on 11 July 1944. It was a smash hit. It was held over for a week. The New York debut was at the Shubert Theatre on 2 August 1944. It ran for 191 performances, closing 13 January 1945. Then it went on tour.

Despite its excellent box office, the critics drubbed it unmercifully. Starting up costs were at $150,000, seats at $4.80, tops then for a musical, which *Catherine* wasn't. All *Variety* could say on 9 August was that "the play lacks fun." The *Herald Tribune* reported on 3 August: "Mae West came to Broadway last night, decked out like a battleship in a swimming pool. . . . Since her script is monotonous, and her acting is more limited than ever, nothing even approaching entertainment emerges. . . ."

Burton Rascoe commented on 3 August in the *World-Telegram* that the audience had purchased $4,000,000 worth of War Bonds in order to attend. He felt the cast had stage fright and noted that Mae herself flubbed half a dozen lines. Ward Morehouse writing for the *New York Sun* thought "as a play it misses badly" and that it was "a wayward and tedious piece." Ed Sullivan acknowledged that Mae West alone could make the play go, and, in truth, she did.

Critics agreed its funniest moments were when Mae burlesqued Catherine. The historical content was unappreciated. She had one song, "Solid, Strong, and Sensational." At least two lovers called on her for each costume worn among several changes. Mae had a curtain speech: "Catherine was a great empress. She also had three hundred lovers. I did the best I could in a couple of hours."

Catherine toured to the National Theatre in Washington. It played four weeks in Chicago, at the Studebaker, the same theatre, incidentally, where that year Gladys George staged an unsuccessful revival of *Personal Appearance*. Mae wanted to avoid another hot summer with the show, so it closed. Included in the itinerary were St. Louis, Kansas City, and a series of one- and two-night stands, ending in Columbus, Ohio, a city always exceedingly warm toward her.

Mae with her 75-pound costume, not counting sceptre or tiara, in *Catharine Was Great*

Shortly after 1946 began, with Mae back in Hollywood, James Timony proposed to J.J. Shubert that Mae should do a new play. Shubert came to Hollywood and worked out a format. He was producing.

CATHERINE WAS GREAT

A COMEDY IN A PROLOGUE AND THREE ACTS BY MAE WEST. PRODUCED BY MICHAEL TODD. STAGED BY ROY HARGRAVE. SETTINGS BY HOWARD BAY. COSTUMES BY MARY PERCY SCHENCK AND ERNEST SCHRAPPS. CHOREOGRAPHY BY MARGARET SANDE.

CAST

Jim   Hubert Long
Mike   Robert Strauss
Greg   Philip Huston
Roy   Mischa Tonken
Corporal Joe   Joel Ashley
Soldiers: Milton Gordon, Carl Bensen, Jack Burke, John Colby, Boyd de Brossard, Anthony Fortune, Eddy Grove, William Skelton, Carl Specht.

IN THE PLAY

Count Nikolai Mirovich   Coburn Goodwin
Captain Dronsky   Philip Cary Jones
English Ambassador   Henry Vincent
Ambassador Choiseul   Owen Coll
Ambassador Murad Pasha   Don de Leo
Captain Danilov   Don Gibson
Alexis Orloff   Hubert Long
Count Panin   Charles Gerrard
Chief Chamberlain   John Stephen
Gregory Orloff   Philip Huston
Catherine II   Mae West
Prince Potemkin   Joel Ashley
Varvara   Elinor Counts
Florian   Ray Bourbon
Lieutenant Bunin   Gene Barry
Marshal Suvorov   John Parrish
Ivan VI   Michael Bey
Pugacheff   Bernard Hoffman
Innkeeper   Harry Bodin
Maurice   Leon Hamilton
Admiral Semechkin   William Malone
Semyonev   Victor Finney
Vanya   Frank Baxter
Chimneysweep   Lester "Red" Towne
Chechkovski   Dayton Lummis
Pageboys   Buddy and Dickie Millard
Ladies-in-waiting: Edna Eckert, Michael Mauree, Mila Niemi, Gloria Pierre, Mary Reid, Gerry Brent.
Councillors: William C. Tubbs, Frank Stevens, Albert Bayne, Joseph Mann, Charles Hart, Robert Morse.
Chamberlains: Michael Spreder, Victor Finney.
Ushers: Dick Ellis, Reginald Allen.
Guards: George Anderson, Eden Burrows, Jerry Lucas, Richard Spohr, Raymond Stenzi, John Frederick.

Admiring her jewelry

The British producer Howard Welch with Mae and and Jim Timony at the Mocambo Club

Mae adapted a play called **Ring Twice Tonight** to her own style. Miles Mander, Fred Schiller, and Thomas Dunphy had written it. A harrowing tour was booked, mostly one-night stands. At fifty-four, Mae, none the worse for her age, apparently, played in fifty-three cities

With Michael Ames and Roy Gordon in *Come On Up*

in eight months. Under its original title, the comedy opened at the Auditorium in Oakland, California, for one day, and then moved on. *Variety* gave it an out-of-town review based on the Oakland premier. "Mae West has returned," the article stated, ". . . to the style of drama that once sent her to the workhouse in Manhattan. . . . Broadway chances are poor."

Shubert very much wanted the play on Broadway following the tour. He responded by running a full page of local reviews favorable to the play in *Variety* on 12 June 1946.

The plot was that of a comic spy thriller with Brazilian Nazis, big-shot steel magnates, racketeers, a whimsical professor of astronomy, two avid sailors, and a congressman. Mae handled her costume changes by disappearing at various intervals through a door ostensibly leading to the bedroom with one or another character. Soon after it was on the road, Mae altered the title to **Come On Up**, which audiences could more readily identify with her.

Refusing to stay in Milwaukee in a hotel, perhaps as a reaction to the Frank Wallace affair, Mae drove each day from Chicago for a total of four performances at the Davidson. The *Milwaukee Sentinel*, a Hearst paper at the time, commented on 26 December 1946: "It cannot be said that **Come On Up** is not on the corny side, but it is cheerful, crude, well-plowed corn, grown that way on purpose. Many women in the audience giggled delightedly while their escorts wriggled with discomfort . . . Miss West's wisecracks are good in spots and almost always seem to be funny when she whips them off." The same sentiment was reflected on 8 July 1946 when Copeland C. Burg wrote in the *Chicago Herald-American*: "We never knew how vulgar we were until we saw Miss West in this new play. Laughing with Miss West may be vulgar, yet it is honest vulgarity, and there's nothing wrong with that."

When *Come On Up* closed at the Biltmore in Los Angeles on 22 February 1947, Jim Timony had plans for a European tour of *Diamond Lil.* On 14 May 1947, *Variety* announced that the dates for the London performance of the play had been set.

COME ON UP

A COMEDY IN TWO ACTS, FOUR SCENES, AND A PRO-LOGUE, BY MILES MANDER, FRED SCHILLER, AND THOMAS DUNPHY. PRODUCED BY SELECT OPERATING CORPORATION. DIRECTED BY RUSSELL FILLMORE. SETTINGS BY ERNEST GLOVER. MISS WEST'S GOWNS BY PETER JOHNSON.

CAST

General Quantillo   Charles La Torre
Krafft   John Doucette
Carliss Dale   Mae West
Jeff Bentley   Michael Ames
Lottie   Cleo Desmond
J.W. Bentley   Roy Gordon
Doug Wade   Charles G. Martin
Annette   Francesca Rotoli
Mike Annegan   Joe McTurk
Professor Twilby   Harold Bostwick
Sailor   Allan Nixon
Lou Baker, Sailor   Harry (The Hipster) Gibson
Nick   Don Harvey
Ramon Rodriguez   Robert Tafur
Senator Carlton   Willis Claire
Larkin   Jon Anton
Bell Captain   John Hampton
Ed   Peter Dunne
Frank   George Spelvin
General Housenborough   Robert Long

(Note: This was the cast as of opening night at Oakland. On the road, the following changes in personnel were made. Todd Andrews replaced Michael Ames. Tom DeGraffen-reid replaced Charles G. Martin. Philip Russell replaced Harold Bostwick. Leonard Marvin replaced Harry Gibson. Scott Davis replaced Peter Dunne. The sailor before Lou Baker was given the credit of "Buddy." For the sake of those who might be interested, below will be found a listing of the playdates of **Come On Up** *on its exhausting tour of the country. First is the date, then the theatre, the city, and the state.)*

Signing autographs for the Boy Scouts

Lil was scheduled for a twelve-week tour of the provinces before settling down in its London run. Mae selected two American leads for the show in Hollywood and recruited the rest of the cast in England. It opened at the Prince of Wales Theatre in London's West End on 24 January 1948. *The Times* (London) reported on 26 January that "Miss West is a competent actress. Appearing in a tawdrily ornate framework of her own devising, she puts across her own kind of audacity with good timing and a shrewd sense of its own absurdity." Leonard Mosley remarked in the *London Daily Telegraph*: ". . . She, herself, is a Restoration comedy rolled into one body—earthy, happy, and outspoken. Shocked me? No, I just liked her." *The New York Times'* correspondent said on 25 January: "The audience displayed little

With Hedda Hopper at VACS benefit fights at Olympic Stadium

interest in the comedy melodrama of the nineties, but it warmed to Miss West. . . ." Mae was in England for ten months, from September, 1947, to May, 1948.

When she returned to Los Angeles, she immediately became embroiled in a law suit claiming $100,000 from her in behalf of two plaintiffs, O'Brien and Kane, who insisted she had stolen ideas about Catherine the Great from their manuscript. Due to the floods which had destroyed her own records, and the fire that had destroyed file copies of her scripts held by The Writers' Club of Hollywood, it was touch and go. The trial lasted seven weeks, from 24 August 1948 until 8 October 1948 and resulted in a hung jury, 7-5 in Mae's favor, insufficient for either side to secure a victory. Mae summed it up in her autobiography, "like many people, they treated me like a bank."

An American revival of **Diamond Lil** opened out of town on 29 November 1948 at Montclair, New Jersey. Brooks Atkinson responded to her performance in *The New York Times* on 30 November 1948: "A fine, full-bosomed woman with lots of glitter and gaudiness, Mae is an original, unclassified phenomenon, about as wicked as a sophomore beer night and smoker. What was all that patrol-wagon rumpus about, twenty years ago?" He felt Mae had "become a part of American folklore, like the minstrel show and burlesque."

The New York opening was at the Coronet Theatre on 5 February 1949. The trade papers gave it, on the whole, a favorable reception. *Variety* ran the cast to the 1928 original in its review of 9 February. Others suggested that the first run was only seventy-eight performances. They got this figure from Burns Mantle's *The Best Plays of 1927-28*. It was wrong. They should have checked the *Billboard* Index of 7 September 1929. Mantle only gave the figures as of his publication date, while the play was still running.

John Chapman of the *Daily News* recalled attending the 1928 premiere. "It didn't even get the second-string reviewers, or the third stringers; it got theatre-loving reporters off the city desks, including me, who were eager to see anything on a pair of passes." In 1949, the play was "an event, with a platoon of cops keeping a big gallery of gawkers across the street. Miss West was hot—much hotter than she was twenty years ago." *Lil*, he said, "had me and the rest of the Coronet Theatre audience laughing fit to—if you'll pardon the expression—bust."

The Pablo part was revised to Juarez; it had been Serge Stanieff in the film version. A few other characters were shifted around or altered. Toward the end of the third act, Mae came down to the footlights and let go with three songs, "Frankie and Johnnie," "Come Up and See Me Sometime," and "After You've Gone." William Hawkins said of the response in the *New York World-Telegram* on 7 February 1949, "if Saturday night's audience had its way, she would still be singing." Hawkins added something I can say it pleases me to quote: "For all this travesty, Miss West is basically a wise woman of the theatre. She has her tricks perfected, but she knows when and where to attract attention. With no more difficulty than breathing, she could take every scene away from her cast. But when she's not talking, she has a composure many more solemn actors could emulate profitably, and beyond that, she watches and listens to the people around her. There is never a moment when you do not wish she would talk or walk or sing more. And the payoff, of course, is that you leave the theatre planning to come right

In the revival of *Diamond Lil*

Steve Cochran, Charles G. Martin, Miriam Goldina in *Diamond Lil*

back for more. Miss West is reported to have made several million dollars out of variations on the role of Lil. I hope she has, because she deserves every one of them."

Richard Watts, Jr., reported in the *New York Post*, "Miss West has come back to town . . . and is to be found putting sex back into its foolish place." Robert Coleman remarked in the New York *Daily Mirror*, "No player in recent seasons has received an ovation such as was given Miss West on her entrance Saturday night. The audience went wild and cheered for several minutes. And the customers kept blistering their palms throughout the evening." Brooks Atkinson reviewed it again for the *Times*, saying, "Although Miss West is the goddess of sex, it might reasonably be argued that she scrupulously keeps sex out of her acting by invariably withdrawing from anything but the briefest encounters."

There were a few negative comments to go with the endorsements. But it was in *Variety* on 9 February 1949 that a critic said something worth framing, especially as it appeared in that tabloid: "It's more than just funny in spots; it's also rather guileless and quaint. If only as an illustration of the inherent folly of censorship, it should be preserved."

DIAMOND LIL (*American revival*)

A Play In Three Acts by Mae West, based, according to Burns Mantle, on a play by Jack Linder. Produced by Albert H. Rosen and Herbert J. Freezer. Staged by Charles K. Freeman. Sets by William DeForest and Ben Edwards. Costumes by Paul DuPont.

Staff for the "Diamond Lil" Company during its almost four-year existence:

General manager Albert H. Rosen
Company manager Irving Becker
General press representative Bill Doll
Company press representative Dick Williams
Stage manager John T. Sloper
Musical contractor David Lapin
Assistant stage manager Mike Keene
Executive secretary Albert H. Lewis
Production secretary Raena Wilka
Master carpenter Larry Berquist
Master electrician Gene Tierney
Assistant electrician William Moran
Master properties Joseph Sola
Wardrobe mistress Hattie Rigby Fabry

CAST

Jim Billy Van
Bill Jack Howard
Porter James Quinn
Ragtime Dick Arnold
Spike George Warren
Jerry Harry Warren
Card Players Fred Catania, Patsy Perroni
Kitty Harriet Nelson
Frances Sheila Trent
Flo Sylvia Syms
Maggie Louise Jenkins
Flynn Charles G. Martin
Kane Mike Keene
Gus Jordan Walter Petrie
Sally Frances Arons
Rita Miriam Goldina
Juarez Steve Cochran
Mike James Fallon
Diamond Lil Mae West
Charlie Peter Chan
Bessie Buddy Millette
Violet Margaret Magennis

Barbara   Marilyn Lowe
Captain Cummings   Richard Coogan
Peter the Duke   Lester Laurence
Doheney   Ralph Chambers
Jacobson   Louis Nussbaum
Chick Clark   Jeff Morrow
Sailor   Jerry Tobias
Cop   F. Ben Miller
Singer   Michael Edwards
Miss West's accompanist   David Lapin
Bowery pianist   Arnold New
Ray   Ray Bourbon
Cyclists, Customers, Bowery Characters, Policemen, Society Women, Society Men: John Quigg, Robert Behr, Frederic Meyer, James Wiler, Robert Allender, William H. Miller, Hiram Breckinridge, Harry Miller, Curtis Karpe, Hyacinth Melon, Ethel Curtis, Lawrence Holmes, Marjorie Dalton, Lucille Perroni, Joli Coleman, Lillian Martin.

Jim Timony wasn't there for the first time in more than twenty years for an opening night. He was entering his final illness.

The mood was right for *Lil*. The impetus of the short tour, the warm public reaction to opening night, the positive reviews, would all have made for a long run. John Chapman of the *Daily News*, whose comments were so encouraging, invited Mae to appear on his first local television show. Mae was to have a police escort to the studio between performances. As she left, Mae's heel caught in a frayed place in a small rug in the powder room at her hotel, and she fell. Her ankle was broken. On 26 February 1949, after only twenty-nine performances, **Diamond Lil** had to be suspended. Some $200,000 in advance ticket sales was refunded. With her foot in a cast, Mae went back to California. The hotel put up a bronze plaque. It reads, "Mae West Slipped Here."

When Mae recovered, she went on the road with *Lil* through what was left of 1949, all of 1950, and a good part of 1951. The show played throughout the entire country. In the summer of 1951, she staged it for limited engagements in the Bronx, Brooklyn, and Queens. On 14 September 1951 it opened for what was designed to be a limited run at the Broadway Theatre, closing 10 November 1951 after sixty-seven performances. The same reviewer who had remarked on censorship in *Variety*, said now on 19 September 1951: "The play was always trash, of course. But Miss West, a personality once regarded as the ultra of sinful sex, has gotten no younger, slimmer, or more subtle . . . In general the evening is a toughie." This is the strange way in the theatre. Accountable only to some obscure, unknown principle, there are right moments and wrong moments. In 1951 for *Lil* on Broadway was a wrong moment; 1949 had been right.

DIAMOND LIL   (*Second Broadway revival*)

A PLAY BY MAE WEST. REVIVED BY GEORGE BRANDT. STAGED BY CHARLES K. FREEMAN.

General manager   William S. Levine
Press   J. Friedman, Lorela Val Mery
Stage managers   Walter Johnson, Patsy Perroni, Lester Laurence

CAST

Jim   Billy Van
Bill   Jack Howard
Ragtime   Arnold New
Card players   Jerry Ford, Les Colodny
Kitty   Linda King
Frances   Sheila Trent
Flo   Helen Waters
Flynn   Charles G. Martin
Kane   Patsy Perroni
Gus Jordan   Walter Petrie
Sally   Alice Martin
Rita   Zoyla Talma
Juarez   James Courtney
Mike   James Fallon
Diamond Lil   Mae West
Charlie   Charles Brown
Bessie   Lois Harmon
Barbara   Marion Gates
Captain Cummings   Dan Matthews
Peter the Duke   Lester Laurence
Jacobson   Louis Nussbaum
Chick Clark   Val Gould
Sailor   Bert Remsen
Dan Darcy   Sid Lawson
Doheney   Harry Kadison
Lefty   Fred Ardath
Miss West's accompanist   David Lapin
Bowery Musicians: Roy Johnson, Willie Creager, Adrian Tei, Bernie Friedland.
Customers, Bowery characters, Policemen, Society Women, Society Men, members of the Salvation Army: Marjery Ardath, Betty Bennett, Clara Cubitt, Gabrielle Gray, Ann Greeley, Lillian Martin, Lucille Perroni, Nellie Ransom, Mildred Ryder, Anne Sorenson, Elsa Tohl, Byron Conner, Guy Costa, Russ Dore, Al Durand, Willis Hidden, Doc Kramer, Lee Madden, Edward Marsh, Bill McElheny, Charles Myron, Mike O'Dowd, Jack Spenelly.

With Hercules

Mae played in summer stock during the warm months of 1952, doing a revival of **Come On Up**. She had hopes of revising a play called **Sextette**, written by Charlotte Francis, an Englishwoman, and which, at Lee Shubert's instigation, she rewrote to suit herself. Jim Timony's condition was worsening. Mae took a house for him at Malibu Beach and devoted herself to her real estate holdings, which he had been managing. She hasn't said much about it, but Mae West has always taken care of her own. She watched over Timony during his last years, as she had once looked after her father.

Mae put together her muscle act in 1954 and opened at the Sahara in Las Vegas. She had seventeen men in the show, nine of them in loincloths. They were weight-lifters. Mae began with the song, "I Wanna Do All Day What I Do All Night." Another of her songs was "Take It Easy, Boys," which Lester Lee wrote for Rita Hayworth in her 1953 Columbia film **Miss Sadie Thompson,** but which censorship deleted. She included Louise Beavers in a skit as her maid, feeding her the line from **I'm No Angel,** "Beulah, peel me a grape." The show ended with a **Diamond Lil** monologue and her rendition of "Frankie and Johnnie." The whole enterprise lasted only thirty-nine minutes. *Variety* reported on 4 August 1954, "In the same Congo

The Las Vegas Muscle Men Act

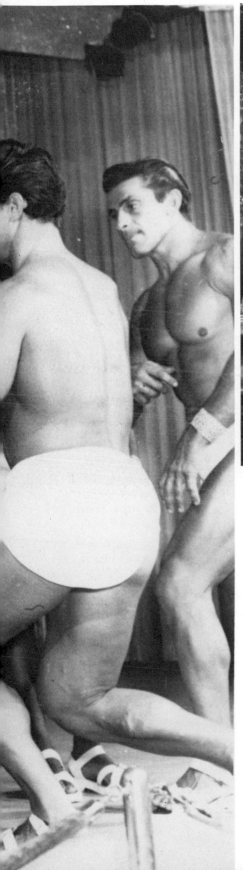

Room that saw the Vegas debut of Marlene Dietrich ten months ago, and the sensation caused by her 'topless' gown, Diamond Lil . . . swayed her ball-bearing hips on a nightclub floor for the first time in her career. Unlike Miss Dietrich, she bares nothing, yet reveals everything."

Mae moved on with the floor show to New York's Latin Quarter, where she broke attendance records, and the Chez Paree in Chicago, hitting only the highest of the high spots. At the Chez Paree, *Variety* reviewed the act on 16 February 1955. "The femme ringsiders," the reviewer said, "give blushing gasps of admiration to the musclemen, while their paunchy and/or anemic escorts cringe before the display of physical excellence. . . ."

Mae continued with the show in short stints until 1959, playing the Italian Village in San Francisco, the Latin Casino in Philadelphia, and a return engagement at the Sahara. In 1955 she recorded some of her hit songs for a Decca album entitled "The Fabulous Mae West," which is still available. One of her muscle boys took up with Jayne Mansfield, inaugurated a lot of unpleasant publicity, and even commenced an abortive lawsuit against her for $100,000. When the

bedraggled show appeared at the Chi Chi in Palm Springs, *Variety* reported on 25 March 1959: "She looks tired, and except for the quartet in tails and top hats who sing and dance the opening commercial dealing with Miss West's sex allure, everybody else in the act looks worn out, too."

Also in March, Mae appeared with Rock Hudson, then a box-office sensation, on the Academy Awards presentation, produced by Jerry Wald. Mae's number, her own setting of "Baby, It's Cold Outside," was a national hit. Her memoirs, which she had been dictating for the last several years, were published that fall by Prentice-Hall.

Mae has done more on television than she got to do on radio. She made an appearance on the Dean Martin show, exchanging quips with Bob Hope, another guest star, sang two songs, and reclined on a chaise lounge while Martin sang her a love ditty. She guested on the Red Skelton show, during its heyday, and showed up in an installment of the situation comedy series, *Mr. Ed*, about a talking horse, for which former cowboy actor Allan "Rocky" Lane did the voice. Her appearance on *Person to Person*, video-taped at her apartment, was cancelled before telecast. CBS was alarmed lest certain things she said "be misconstrued" and place them in the position of NBC after the

Scenes (with Charles Collingwood) from a "Person to Person" television program which was cancelled.

Chase & Sanborn Hour. When interviewer Charles Collingwood remarked on all the mirrors in her bedroom, a desire Mae realized in the thirties after conceiving of it in *The Constant Sinner*, she replied, "They're for personal observation. I always like to know how I'm doin'." *TV Guide* ran a feature article on her suite, with several color photographs. Unfortunately, Mae was still too outspoken for the television audience. When Collingwood asked her about foreign affairs, she responded in a sultry voice, "I've always had a weakness for foreign affairs."

On 7 July 1961 Mae opened at the Edgewater Beach Playhouse in Chicago, in her stage production of *Sextette*. Henry Guettell, the theatre manager, was also the producer. After two weeks at the Edgewater, the play was scheduled for the Northland Playhouse in Detroit, and then a week each at Warren and Columbus, Ohio. *Variety* on 5 July 1961 quoted Mae as saying that she planned to take the show to Broadway. Alan Marshal and Jack LaRue were in the cast. Aaron Frankel was the director.

The play was plagued with difficulties. Casting problems delayed rehearsals until only a week before it was to open. Then Mae came down with laryngitis and the first three performances had to be cancelled. Under-rehearsed at its belated premiere, the critics panned the show for its missed cues and prompting from the wings, although they spoke enthusiastically of Mae. On 8 July, during the matinee performance, Alan Marshal suffered a fatal heart attack. His son Kit, also in the cast, requested that the show go on.

Henry Guettel took over as a temporary replacement, doing his

Clowning with Red Skelton In 1968

love scenes with script in hand. Tom Conway, once famous as The Falcon at RKO, down on his luck and drinking heavily, was flown in to take Marshal's part. He read the script and departed the same day. *Variety* commented on 19 July 1961: "The Edgewater was unable to sell a single theatre party for the show, and it goes down as the silo's biggest box-office flop to date."

By the time **Sextette** made it to Detroit, Francis Bethencourt had taken over as Mae's leading man. After the Ohio engagements, the play moved to Miami Beach at the Coconut Grove Playhouse. Then Mae closed it, running a full page advertisement in *Variety* on 27 September 1961, as Shubert had once done, reproducing favorable reviews.

The story concerned an American movie star recently married to a young British baronet who learns he's her sixth husband. Jack LaRue was the ghost of No. 5, and evidently caused a laugh riot with audiences. Mae West is the only person in all the industry to have properly appreciated the natural comic talent in LaRue; his aptitude was totally wasted in Hollywood in gangster roles. Michael Fox was her Hungarian ex-husband, who wanted to get her to make movies in Italy with Kit Marshal, a new screen sensation. Bard Olson played Mae's agent. Wink Hess said in his column for the *Columbus Citizen-Journal*, "Without Mae, it could not really exist. For, like it says in the play, she is an American institution. And the legendary high priestess of sex in the wisecracking, frankly ribald manner did not disappoint the paying customers." The play was Mae's last legitimate stage vehicle.

" 'That Saint Paul,' Rinaldi said.
'He was a rounder and a chaser
and then when he was no longer
hot he said it was no good.
When he was finished he made
the rules for us that are still
hot'."
—*Ernest Hemingway in*
A FAREWELL TO ARMS

The Legend of Mae West

She's said it many times. In real life Miss West is not the person she appears to be in her public performances. The legendary Mae West is a created, synthetic folk figure. It's not a new image. It's reminiscent of the Aphrodite.

A *humor* is a pure type. A person is all bad or all good, never in-between. Humors are therefore the essence of melodrama. Despite an overwhelming thrust from modern literature to the contrary, humors persist everywhere. You cannot expect a humor to be a real person, subject to foibles, weaknesses, vanities, untoward cravings, spontaneous generosities, capricious good will, unrepentant pettiness, self-righteousness. A story peopled by humors can tell you nothing of life and human beings. I think that's the primary reason they're popular.

The young Mae West knew men well. She exploited the vanities and hypocrisies surrounding sexuality and rose to notoriety. By the time she entered films, her social critique, bitter and poignant on stage, was diluted somewhat through her constant use of the Diamond Lil characterization as a humor. The attacks of the censors cut out more than sexual innuendoes. Their restrictions deprived the vehicle of her social commentary. This limitation left Mae with a Diamond Lil made mute. She was billed and recognized increasingly as a sex goddess. She willingly became what the public insisted they wanted her to be, and what censorship would allow her to be.

I have found no "inside story" on Mae West. Thre are those who point to her present state of self-insulation, the aura of a Hollywood star from the golden era with which she has surrounded herself, and chalk it up to offensive egotism. I approach all such considerations with indifference. It is sufficient that she is living as best suits her temperament.

"I'm my own original creation," she remarked in her *Playboy* interview. ". . . I concentrate on myself most of the time; that's the only way a person can become a star in the true sense. I never wanted a love that meant surrender of my self-possession. I saw what it did to other people when they loved another person the way I loved myself, and I didn't want that problem. I had to stay in command of my career."

As for Mae's social criticism, the first of her dangerous notions was her effort to explode the myth of male supremacy. A man could make love to several women. Among the Mormons for a time, a man could even maintain several wives. But should a woman dare have more than one man, society condemned her as a strumpet. Mae reacted. If having sexual relations with several men meant a woman was a strumpet, then she would glorify harlotry. Little harm can come from sexual promiscuity compared with destruction of war.

The Western world has always held curious notions about women. The ancient Greeks regarded women as basically frivolous creatures, less than men in intelligence and all other attributes. The subsequent influence of Hebrew teachings and Christianity altered this image. Woman was an evil temptress. Eve led Adam into sin and out of Paradise. St. Paul taught that while it was better to fornicate than to burn, it was best to pursue a celibate life. St. Jerome, St. Augustine, and other early Church fathers amplified this distrust of women, disapproved of lust, and warned of the curse of the flesh. By the age of Victoria, a long tradition had come about that split women into the virtuous ones, symbolized by the virgin Isis and the Virgin Mary, and the evil ones, descended from Eve, who throughout history have appealed solely to man's "lower" instincts.

Mae set many of her stories in the Victorian era. Her heroines were women who knew the duplicity of men and refused to be enmeshed by them. Frequently her heroines turned male hypocrisy and double standards into advantages. Her heroines knew the difference between sexual urgency and dependency, and that men tend to merge them into what convention calls love. They surrendered physically, but withheld the satisfaction of mental domination. They distinguished between sexuality, which is a biological need, and physical possession, which is an ego need. Mae's women compel men to admire them.

When I was asked to speak at a university recently, somebody in the audience asked me to tell him in what Mae's attraction for homosexuals consists. There was one answer I thought of immediately. A number of critics who should know better insist that Mae isn't a woman at all but a skillful female impersonator. For what it's worth as a reply, I have reproduced Mae's marriage certificate. Wisconsin is a difficult state in which to be wed and it is unlikely in the extreme that Mae could have succeeded in falsifying her sex before receiving medical clearance.

Mae has a better answer than this. "I've always had it, dear," she said of her fascination for inverts. "They're crazy about me 'cause I give 'em a chance to play. My characterization is sexy and with humor and they like to imitate me, the things I say, the way I say 'em, the way I move. It's easy for 'em to imitate me 'cause the gestures are exaggerated, flamboyant, *sexy*, and that's what they wanna look like, feel like, and I've stood up for 'em. They're good kids. I don't like the police abusin' 'em, and in New York I told 'em, 'When you're hittin' one of those guys, you're hittin' a woman,' 'cause a born homosexual is a female in a male body." Mae has always slanted her acts to appeal to women even more than to men, and many of her most avid followers and fans to this day are women.

Mae West has done her work well in behalf of liberating attitudes toward sexuality. She regards it as wholly natural and healthy. To this extent, she has opposed the repressive measures of organized religion. In the portrait of life in her early films, she shows evil as the inspiration or result of destructive behavior, harmful to others. Sexuality, when it is enjoyed freely, hurts no one and is to be considered one of the genuinely good things in life.

Egotism and fame, wealth and success are natural effects of the Mae West life-style. "My basic style I never changed," she has remarked. "I couldn't if I wanted to. I am a captive of myself. It or I created a Mae West and neither of us could let the other go, or would want to." Like Ruby in **Belle of the Nineties**, she might comment on her popularity, "That's funny, 'cause I don't know how to cook."

Mae West in her career has aroused vituperation in a great many quarters. It must be attributed more to her ideas than to her exploitation of sex. She has never been guilty of what is termed indecent exposure; in fact, most of the time she has been overdressed by contemporary standards. She lost her battle with the censors, but it was a battle she knew she would lose from the beginning. Mae West's comedy at its finest belongs to an enlightened future when humanity, having lost a totally undesirable, pretentious, and feigned innocence, will have learned not to take itself, nor its judgments and opinions, quite so seriously.

At the premiere of *Myra Breckinridge*, greet-her fans.